ALL WORK AND NO PLAY?

WITHDRAWN

ALL WORK AND NO PLAY?

A STUDY OF WOMEN AND LEISURE

ROSEMARY DEEM

OPEN UNIVERSITY PRESS
Milton Keynes · Philadelphia

Open University Press
Open University Educational Enterprises Limited
12 Cofferidge Close
Stony Stratford
Milton Keynes MK11 1BY, England

and

242 Cherry Street
Philadelphia, PA 19106, USA

First Published 1986

British Library Cataloguing in Publication Data
Deem, Rosemary
    All work and no play?: the sociology of
    women and leisure.
    1. Leisure—Social aspects—Great Britain
    2. Women—Great Britain—Recreation
    I. Title
    306'.48'088042   GV183

    ISBN 0-335-15355-0
    ISBN 0-335-15354-2 Pbk

Library of Congress Cataloging in Publication Data
Main entry under title:

Deem, Rosemary.
    All work and no play?

    Bibliography: p.
    Includes index.
    1. Women—Recreation.   2. Leisure.   3. Women—
Great Britain—Recreation.   4. Leisure—Great Britain.
I. Title.
GV183.D44 1986   790.1'94   86-8651
ISBN 0-335-15355-0
ISBN 0-335-15354-2 (pbk.)

Text design by Nicola Sheldon
Typeset by Gilbert Composing Services, Leighton Buzzard
Printed in Great Britain by St. Edmundsbury Press, Bury St. Edmunds,
Suffolk.

Contents

Acknowledgements

I should like to thank Jill Day, Mary Maynard and Kevin Brehony for their encouragement and helpful comments on earlier drafts. My analysis of women's leisure has benefitted enormously from the discussions which took place in 1981 at a series of seminars on 'Women, sport, leisure and education', held at the Open University, the 1984 International Leisure Studies Conference at Brighton, the 1985 'Women, leisure and well-being' workshop weekend at the Centre for Leisure Research, Dunfermline College of P.E. and meetings of the ESRC/Sports Council Steering Group on the Sheffield Polytechnic 'Women and Leisure' project. I have also learnt a great deal from Chris Griffin, and from one of my research students Sheila Scraton who has pioneered the contemporary analysis of girls and school P.E. Finally I am indebted to many women in Milton Keynes who helped with the research on which parts of this book are based and the School of Education Research committee at the Open University which funded that research.

List of Tables

CHAPTER ONE

Do women have leisure?

---

1. Why Women's Leisure?

My interest in a sociological analysis of sport and leisure began when I was an undergraduate student; there can't be many sociology students whose BA dissertation was written on the sociology of show jumping. My particular interest in the position of women also dates from the same period in the late 1960s when coming to higher education from the protected environment of a single-sex grammar school, I was surprised to find that male students regarded their female peers as intellectual inferiors. My concern about the situation of women was increased when a (male) tutor asked me to write an essay on 'Why women don't want to work' a title which both then and now incensed me with its brutal insensitivity as to the nature and extent of the work tasks undertaken by women. Subsequently, involvement with the women's movement and with both an academic and political study of women's education, led to an interest in the manner in which girls and women are prepared for and live their gender-divided lives. But whereas women's schooling was one of the first topics to which the newly developing field of women's studies turned its attention, leisure and sport have been one of the last, despite the existence for example of clear links between education and leisure. Partly this neglect has been because of the legacy of male leisure researchers, insisting that leisure was something struggled over by male employees. But it is also attributable to the lesser importance women (as opposed to men) attach to leisure, and to the belief that leisure is a luxury or optional extra. Moving to a new town apparently overflowing with 'provided' leisure facilities quickly made me realize that such facilities were much less used by women, and so began a study which explored what women thought about leisure and in what leisure activities they participated. Only slowly did it dawn on me that there were severe difficulties with the concept of leisure itself (briefly searching for an

1

alternative concept brought only such non-words as 'lurk' or 'worksure' to mind). This apart, there are many good reasons for studying women's leisure, of which these are just a few, but important ones:

a) to help us understand what the relationship is between work and play in women's lives
b) to enable an exploration of the factors and constraints which operate on women's leisure
c) to appreciate the variety of women's lifestyles and the interests and pursuits from which they gain enjoyment
d) to help improve the lives of women and their position in society, so that they too become entitled to relaxation and recreation

It has become fashionable amongst some leisure researchers to argue that leisure is actually just a tool of capitalist societies, which can be used to encourage greater consumption of goods and services, or which can be offered to the unemployed as 'compensation' for the absence of paid work and an adequate income (Clarke and Critcher 1985). It would be foolish to entirely dismiss such arguments, since there is, as we shall see, some truth in them. However we should not allow such debates to distract our attention from the very crucial role of leisure in allowing people to relax, improve their physical and mental well-being and enjoy themselves by escaping from their many paid and unpaid tasks and cares which form a large part of our everyday existence. Whether what is available to individuals in their leisure time is adequate or exploitative is of course a very major concern and one to which the book will return many times. But the *right* to leisure is in many ways a prior concern for women and it is to the ways in which leisure for women is perceived, structured and experienced that much of my analysis will be directed. This introductory chapter will consider the ways in which industrialization has shaped women's lives and leisure; look briefly at what that leisure consists of and where it takes place; examine some of the different perspectives from which women's leisure may be studied; explore the kinds of methodological issues which arise in researching women's lives and finally discuss the key question of how leisure is defined, something which is inescapably present in the study of female leisure and which must simultaneously be both grappled with and held in abbeyance , if it is not to absorb all the energy and attention devoted to studying the what, when, how and why of women's 'free' time.

Subsequently I shall go on to look at some of the findings from a piece of research I did in Milton Keynes in the early 1980s. The study is not a representative nor typical one, for reasons that will be explained later, but it is useful for providing the reader with the 'flavour' of women's leisure, before embarking on the later chapters with their more detailed analysis of particular leisure contexts and content and factors which influence the amount, character and experience of leisure for women. Chapter Three examines leisure in the community, while Chapter Four considers the issues surrounding women's low participation in sport and Chapter Five explores the nature of and constraints on, leisure in the household. Chapter Six is about the relationship between employment, unemployment and how time is allocated to leisure, paid and unpaid work. Chapter Seven discusses the ways in which the stages of life cycles women experience influence their leisure. The final chapter summarizes some of the major points about women's leisure made in the book and looks at the kinds of changes which are necessary if the present balance between women's work and play is to be altered.

As is always the case with newly developing lines of enquiry, there is, as yet, relatively little research which focuses specifically on women's leisure. It will take several years, or even a decade, before we have available to us the body of evidence now available about other aspects of women's experiences, such as education or housework. Even though the ESRC/Sports Council Joint Panel on Leisure Research has commissioned two studies, one on women and leisure in Sheffield and the other in leisure in the home (although the latter is not confined solely to women) it will require many more analyses of different regions and different kinds of women than this to establish a comprehensive knowledge of how gender affects leisure. In this book therefore, whilst I shall draw heavily on national survey material about leisure in general and on the available specific studies (principally my own research in Milton Keynes, the ESRC/Sports Council study of Sheffield being conducted by Green, Hebron and Woodward, and a national study of women and bingo which also involved a community study of a district of Leeds by Dixey and Talbot) I shall also utilize studies whose main objectives have been the study of phenomena other than leisure, or which have focused on women's lives more generally. At the same time it would be foolish to think that it is possible to make generalizations and statements about women's leisure which are not to some degree speculative. The book will pose many questions which are not answerable from our present state of knowledge. But it will also try from the available evidence, to sketch out some of the parameters of the important issues and debates, and explore from what we already know, the ways in which leisure time fits into women's lives.

2. Industrialization and women's leisure

Many texts which explore the issues surrounding leisure begin with or include a piece on the history of leisure. Mostly these deal, sometimes in a very sophisticated way, with the connections between leisure and industrialization, tracing the gradual shift amongst working class males from the interwoven work/leisure pattern of feudal Britain, to the separated work/leisure routines of a society in which paid employment is separated from the home and leisure.

Thompson's (1967) classic essay on time, work, discipline and capitalism focuses on the relationship between industrialization, work, leisure and time for the male working class, and says nothing about the parallel influences of women's conceptions of time, work and leisure imposed by both capitalist and other power structures, including patriarchy (that is, forms of male dominance over women). In particular, it makes the assumption that capitalism altered on a once-and-for-all basis, the perception and notation of time, in moving from irregular and imprecise time based on daylight and night-time, seasonability and task-orientation, to a concept of time which is measured precisely, is controlled by owners of means of production and clearly demonstrates different parts of the day, week and year according to whether work is being done or not. But the fragmented and irregular notion of time which Thompson speaks of as preindustrial, lingering on only in some rural communities and societies, lingers on too for many women, because their unpaid work (especially housework) has only indirect modes of control and no clearly demarcated end or beginning. Hence men's notions of what constitutes a working day and women's notions of this may be very different. For example a recent study by Sixsmith (in Brock 1985) found that some unemployed men would refuse to do housework after 5 pm because that time marks the end of the (paid) working day. Burns' (1973) essay on the history of leisure in industrial societies also focuses on male work and leisure, looking at the struggle for a ten-hour working day and its implications for the commercialization of leisure pursuits. Yet no such major trade union-type struggle to limit the houseworker's day has ever been mounted (except by feminists); even the 'wages for housework campaign' focused on payment more than on limiting the hours or tasks involved. Burns talks about the development of structures of leisure as though these now apply to everyone, whereas in fact such structures (for instance paid holidays, regulation of working hours etc.) apply mainly to those engaged in full time employment. Both Burns and Thompson (1967) provide one foundation for the leisure studies perspective which sees employment and leisure as closely linked. No one denies that this link exists (see Chapter 6), but for many women it is not the *only* relevant link.

Yet there is scarcely any documentation of how industrialization affected women's leisure, although studies such as Liddington's (1984) biography of a Lancashire mill girl and Llewelyn Davies's reprinted work (1977, 1978) on the Women's Cooperative Guild in the late nineteenth century, provide some insights into how working class women organized their lives and leisure. Fletcher (1984) offers an excellent account of the history of the training of women physical education teachers. This history is an important aspect of understanding the nature and extent of women's participation in sport, very relevant to piecing together a history of how industrialization has influenced women's leisure. We know very little about the leisure of bourgeois women in the late eighteenth and nineteenth centuries, although Hall (1982) and Davidoff (1979) have pointed out the mythology of the work/home separation notion for women of this class since bourgeois women's work remained at home. Hall (1982) points out however, that this separation of work and home for men meant women were increasingly cut off from public activities which their menfolk engaged in, with their social life becoming dependent on religious or philanthropic groups and kin. Bourgeois women had servants to undertake their housework but the supervision of these and the care of children still took up much time (Hall 1982), leaving less than might be supposed for leisure, even though the popular view says otherwise.

The twentieth century history of male leisure as so far written is as preoccupied as the nineteenth century accounts, with struggles to limit hours of paid employment and to procure holidays. It also deals with discussions about changes to male team sports, and the inexorable progress of bureaucratization and commercialization of leisure. Again there is little which is directly and centrally relevant to women, until the more recent documentation of the contemporary women's movement (Coote and Campbell, 1982) about the struggles women have faced in their very different lives. Biographies offer some partial and class-specific sources of evidence (Brittain, 1979, 1980) but there is clearly an enormous gap in our knowledge here about how and in what ways the processes that affected men's leisure also affected women's leisure and about those processes specific to women's lives. Whilst men are frequently discussed and depicted as consumers of all kinds of goods and services, many of them relevant to leisure (cars, sports goods, leisure facilities etc.) only teenage females have usually been seen as consumers of other than household necessities or clothes. Similarly, the *sexual* division of labour's impact on women's lives and leisure has been much less researched than the *social* (that is mental/manual) division of labour's impact on men's lives. The modern women's movement has highlighted the disadvantaged position of many women *vis-a-vis* men and contributed significantly to women's increased self-awareness, as well as to sex discrimination legislation. But leisure has scarcely been a high priority for the women's movement, although related struggles for equality at work and in education are clearly relevant to leisure, as are moves to reduce the unequal division of household work.

There is still a great deal to be learnt about how women have, do and could organize their lives around different dimensions of work, non-work and leisure. This relates not only to further historical and theoretical work, but also closely to the question of how one might research women's leisure.

3. The context and content of women's leisure

Women's leisure, insofar as it exists, does not occur in a cultural or economic vacuum. The locations for that leisure are extremely varied, from the home to bingo halls and health clubs, and from lunch-breaks at work to swimming pools and theatres, and in this respect many notions of leisure resources and provision are too narrowly focused. (Deem 1985b). Many factors affect women's leisure interests, access to leisure and leisure experiences, including obvious things like confidence and whether they have an independent income, to less obvious influences like state of health and the leisure interests of any dependent children. Leisure cannot necessarily be equated with 'doing something constructive' and a number of researchers have noted that women especially those with young children or adult dependents may engage in periods of what appear to consist of 'doing nothing' (Hobson 1981, Green, Hebron and Woodward 1985b) although it is unlikely that this *is* the case. But 'low activity' is only one feature of women's leisure; another notable characteristic is that women's leisure frequently has to be slotted into spaces or locations determined by the leisure, work, needs and demands made by others (partners, dependent relatives or children). Furthermore leisure often occurs simultaneously with work activities (watching TV whilst ironing, talking to friends at work, walking through a park on the way to the shops) or is indistinguishable from work (knitting, sewing, gardening, cooking are all activities which might be work or might be leisure and may well on occasions be both at the same time). As Talbot has noted (1981) in summarizing research findings:

> Not only do fewer women than men participate in leisure activities but women also participate in a narrower range of activities, and

watch sport, both live and on television, less than men . . . when data from surveys which include informal leisure activity are added to the knowledge gained from family and community studies, there emerges a picture of home-based, domestic leisure for women, especially for those from the lower socio-economic groups. (Talbot 1981, p.35)

But of course generalizations are just that—not all women fit into this pattern, and there are women, especially young employed, single females, whose leisure interests and concerns are not home-based nor less active than their male counterparts. Nor is it the case that all women find leisure time hard to come by; as Duquemin (1982) found in a study of older women, there was plenty of time in their lives for leisure, and for some, social isolation rather than lack of privacy was a major problem. Women who experience redundancy may also find 'time on their hands' (Martin and Wallace 1984). Nevertheless a common constraint experienced by large numbers of women, whatever their age or marital and employment status, is that of male control, both on an individual basis (husbands or partners controlling where 'their' women go) and through the fears generated in women by collective male control over female sexuality (symbolized by, for example, sexual harassment, rape and assault of women in public and private places). This is substantiated by a number of researchers (Stanley 1981, Deem 1982a, 1982b, Green Hebron and Woodward 1985a and 1985b). So whereas factors such as location, social class, money and interest are likely to have most influence on where men spend their out-of-home leisure time, for women 'safe' out-of-home leisure spent alone or with female friends or relatives generally means going where there are other women, good transport, and few or no men. 'Public' or community leisure then, is less available to women than to men. Additionally some of what appears to be women's out-of-home leisure may be nothing of the sort. When I was researching leisure-centre use in Milton Keynes, I found that many of the women ostensibly 'using' such centres were not actually doing so—they were accompanying their children, who were the main users of the facilities provided (Deem 1982).

Time budget studies are one, although a much-criticized, source of evidence about the context and content of women's leisure. Recent studies suggest that for both sexes, leisure is likely to occur at particular times of the day or week, with evenings and weekends being most 'leisure filled', even for those without paid work, although the ratio of leisure to non-leisure is different for women and men, and varies by employment status (Wyatt 1985). But it is also easy to see that weekends and evenings cannot be a source of leisure for everyone. Some people (not unusually women with children, whose partners have day jobs) may have jobs then, and others, especially women, have to facilitate the leisure of others in their households at those times. Similarly holidays may look as though they are leisure for all, but as women in my Milton Keynes study found, cheap holidays often involve a degree of self-catering (camping, caravanning, holiday flats or houses) and many of the chores associated with normal housework (Deem 1982a 1982b). All this adds up to the inescapable conclusion that women's leisure is much more constrained than men's and occurs relatively less often in proportion to work, whilst taking rather different forms and occurring in different locations and contexts.

4. Perspectives on leisure

Perspectives are not simply an academic indulgence; they are important because they help decide whose leisure gets studied and what kinds of leisure are worth studying, as well as how research is carried out. They also inform the kinds of leisure that are available and provided, and shape policies about leisure and sport. So if leisure policy makers believe leisure is most important to male workers and unemployed youths, and hold stereotyped views about the most appropriate social roles for women, then the policies they design and implement are likely to reflect those views. There is not the time or space here to offer a comprehensive over-view of all the different perspectives on women's and men's leisure, and indeed others have already done this much better than I could (Talbot 1979, Rojek 1985). But what I do want to do is to examine four approaches, one of which (leisure studies) is fortunately fading, one (the feminist) is gradually becoming more important, one because it contrasts with the feminist perspective yet focuses on women, and the final perspective one which is on a rising tide of theoreticism, yet misses some of the political issues from which the study of leisure can only be disentangled at the risk of throwing the baby out with the bath water.

The leisure studies perspective

This approach is on the wane, although its proponents still pop up at academic gatherings and its messages live on. It is a perspective which is mostly atheoretical, sees and researches leisure as though it were a male or unisex phenomenon, which utilizes large scale surveys and often separates leisure from its wider context, although the history of leisure in industrialization is sometimes used. Women whose leisure is unlike those of the males mostly studied are seen as a deviant case and as a problem but not as a very significant problem. Real leisure is about men and male pursuits (Dunning and Sheard 1979, Parker 1971) and gender a new and rather suspicious characteristic which is not yet ready to take its place alongside class and paid employment or capitalism. Insofar as women have been admitted to this perspective it is usually within the context of the family (Smith, Parker and Smith 1973, Parker 1976) rather than in their own right. Both in terms of definitions of leisure (which hinge on connections to paid work) and in terms of methodology few strides have been made in the leisure studies approach, although it has spawned a new breed of personnel, usually besuited males, called 'leisure consultants'. Some of those whose background is in leisure studies have moved more rapidly into the 'discovery' of gender, albeit still in pluralistic vein—another variable added in, (e.g. Roberts, 1981) and have started to reconsider their analyses in this light. Others perhaps hope that factors like gender and race will go away, leaving them free to concentrate on white male leisure once more. Whilst it is not worth taking up more time to discuss the leisure studies perspective, it may help those who are new to the field to realize why it is necessary for those interested in women's leisure to draw heavily on studies whose main focus is something other than leisure for their information and ideas.

Leisure and capitalism; the heavy male theory perspective

Unlike the leisure studies approach, this perspective is on the upward climb. Also unlike the first perspective, much of what it has to say is important (Clarke and Critcher 1985, Fergusson and Mardle 1981). But it is focused primarily on male leisure and male concerns, although it does make concessions in the direction of gender and even race. The main concern of the approach is to look at the connections between leisure and capitalism and it has taken as its jumping off point the increasing debate about 'leisure societies' which seem to be a feature of periods of high unemployment (Horne 1985). The leisure studies approach is critiqued for its atheoreticism, its pluralism and its failure to see leisure as part of a wider culture. So far, so good. But in the re-analysis which follows such critiques, one of the pre-occupations is to show how people are 'duped' by leisure in capitalist societies. What is seen as privatized and personal is commercialized or results from state intervention, is about increasing consumption and is often bureaucratically organized or hightly stylized. Leisure displays the same inequalities as other features of capitalist society; policies to increase participation are misguided and shot through with the dominant ideologies of capitalist society (Clarke and Critcher 1985). Leisure is seen as 'compensation' for the unemployed (Carrington and Leaman 1983). Whilst emphasizing the defects of contemporary leisure, any of its merits are usually lost, despite the stress on the importance of leisure to culture. The emphasis on theoretical argument, whilst taking some account of empirical research, does not see what actually happens to people in their leisure time as its major enterprise (Rojek 1985). Reformist strategies for improving access to leisure are seen as playing into the hands of capitalists and nothing short of a revolutionary transformation of society will do instead. I have some sympathy with the arguments advanced by this approach, because it is the case that some forms of leisure and some kinds of provision, take more account of the profits to be made than the individual user or participant, and that leisure patterns and experiences display the same inequalities as other aspects of contemporary society, like unemployment, welfare benefits or wage differentials. But capitalism is not the only factor responsible for this (what about partriarchy or racism?), nor is it the case that nothing can be changed short of a major transformation of our society. Furthermore, important as theory is, it will not solve the problems of leisure access nor, unless it incorporates factors like gender and race relations fully rather than adding them on like bolt-on components, will it even help us to understand the leisure experiences and constraints of disadvantaged groups. The other major failing of this approach is that, like the leisure studies approach of which it is so critical, it still starts with the 'male as norm' premise which no amount of 'tinkering' with gender or race alters. The third approach does at least start with the notion that women are central, although it has other disadvantages.

The Non-feminist perspective on women's life styles

This approach focuses only on women, but unlike feminist approaches does not attempt to construct any arguments about improving the position of women in society. One writer who has taken this line is Gregory (1982). Gregory is not concerned about whether women are oppressed, but about the need to examine how women's lives are characterized by (p. 52) 'frequently changing lifestyles with integrated work and leisure'. Gregory argues that women have made significant steps in setting up (p. 52) 'values and cultures which benefit themselves and society'. Analysing these may help us to understand how others' lives might be altered to take account of future social, economic and cultural change. Reform is needed, Gregory argues, not because women are exploited, but because their life styles are subject to change according to their stage in the life cycle, and (p. 49) 'the resources required for flexibility and change in any sector of society are greater than those which would maintain lifestyles over larger sections of the life style . . . these resources have often not been available or accessible (because of) . . . political decisions, about resource allocation, the organisations of society and ignorance about what is needed'. She concludes that our starting point in analysing women's leisure should be (p. 52) 'the collective achievement and enjoyment of women to date rather than their failure to slip from under the yoke of male "oppression"'. She thus accepts that women may be exploited, that their lives are different from those of men's, and that a different organization of society, and resources may be required to enable women to make the best use of their potential, but does not see these as either research or social priorities. Unlike the classic leisure studies approach she does at least recognize the need to examine leisure as part of a whole lifestyle rather than as something separate and 'measurable'. But as an approach it has serious limitations because it fails to offer any real explanatory grip on *why* women's lives are different from those of men, and does not engage with the politics of women's leisure as a central issue.

Feminist perspectives

One important point which needs to be made at the outset is that there is no *one* feminist approach. Although all feminists would agree that women are oppressed, they would certainly have disagreements about the determinants of that oppression and the mechanisms through which it operates as well as the strategies for change. So to say an approach is feminist is to say that it places women at the forefront of its analysis and sees them as an oppressed group with certain experiences and interests in common. Feminist perspectives also emphasize the importance of linking analysis and theory to political action and change, something none of the other three perspectives examined put forward as their *raison d'etre*. Furthermore, feminist approaches do not make that neat separation which male researchers and writers are apt to make between their theoretical and empirical analysis of other people and the politics of their own lives and practices. The 'personal is the political' slogan of the contemporary women's movement is an important and crucial distinction between feminist and non-feminist approaches. Feminists have also thought long and hard about the ways in which they research women, a topic I shall return to shortly. I refer here to only two writers as examples of feminist perspectives, but I regard my own research and that of the two other major studies on which this book draws, Green, Hebron and Woodward (1985a and 1985b) in their Sheffield research, and Dixey and Talbot (1982) in their study of Leeds and bingo, as falling firmly within these perspectives.

Stanley's (1980) starting point is to emphasize the personal nature of leisure and the importance of using ethnographic research to study it. This approach, says Stanley, can offer insights into the meaning of leisure (and work) for women. Women, she stresses, are not a leisure 'problem' nor a corporate body about which wide generalizations can be made. Age, education, ethnic origin, possession or non-possession of a driving licence, geographical location, sexual orientation and activity, and leisure interests of friends and lovers are all aspects of women's lives which may divide women from each other. Nevertheless there are certain common constraints which women may experience, for example those deriving from housework and the division of labour; fragmented days, which rule out spending hours on one particular leisure activity only and the need to define and construct leisure so that it fits into the vagaries of care for small children or a seven-day working week. Another commonly shared constraint on women's leisure is seen to be the 'policing' of women's presence in public places by men, which often ensures either that women alone or with other women are not tolerated, or that women have to behave in circumscribed ways (not being out late at night, avoiding eye contact with men, not going to certain places). It is not, Stanley indicates, enough to focus on how women interpret and construct leisure experiences since there also needs to be (p. 35) 'a requirement to investigate all aspects of all women's experiences of all facets of social reality'. Stanley, then, suggests that women do have leisure, but that such leisure is a very personal 'thing' whose meaning must be integrated into the meanings of other aspects of women's experiences and lives. It must be studied sensitively and not in isolation.

Griffin's (1981, 1985) approach differs from Stanley's in its firmer concern with class. She emphasizes the centrality of men to women's leisure, something also stressed by Stanley, for whom male patriarchal power over women is central but which is seen by Griffin as a major aspect of the meaning of leisure and its possibilities and an important axis for leisure activities or leisure time. Griffin claims that gender is a central structuring relation for leisure (although recognizing that class and ethnicity are also important) and sees women's access to and experience of leisure as very restricted. Her work on young women (most fully set out in Griffin 1985) leads her to suggest that for such women, although in different ways

> their primary work/obligation is men; finding a man, keeping him, servicing his work and his leisure, having sex with him on his terms, having his children and taking the 24 hour child-care responsibiity for them (1981, p. 122)

She goes on to suggest that women are both leisure for men and essential to men's leisure:

> Women are an integral part of men's leisure, as 'escorts' whether paid or unpaid, or in relation to the myriad ways in which women must present and construct themselves for men, both materially and psychologically (1981, p. 122)

She also points out that women service men's leisure activities, by undertaking domestic work and childcare, so that men are free to go out to the pub or to have leisure time out of the house. She further notes that many sites where men's leisure takes place are barred or made unattractive to women (football, rugby, working men's clubs, many pubs) by admitting them on male terms. Class is for Griffin a major element in leisure too, because this, like gender, structures and filters peoples' actions and experiences. Working class women unable to earn high wages or get jobs are more likely to be dependent on men than middle class women. However, male relations of power affect all female leisure according to Griffin. Men see leisure as a right; women do not and are not encouraged by men so to do. To the extent that women do engage in leisure, they do so in ways which are largely determined by men and on terms inferior to those enjoyed by men.

This brief overview of some of the perspectives on women's leisure does not do justice to the full range of approaches, but does I think show the importance of taking gender and male–female power relationships into account. While it is tempting to think of drawing on a number of different perspectives, this does risk losing sight of the importance of gender and women's subordinate position in society to any analysis of their leisure, and it is precisely this which is so essential. I want now to go on to consider some of the ways in which women's leisure might be researched.

5. Feminist methodology and the study of female leisure

A major debate now exists about whether certain methods of research are more appropriate to use by feminists than others. Two aspects of this debate are particularly apposite; whether qualitative or quantitative data are best suited to a feminist analysis and whether there are particular methods of research which should be used. The debate is relevant to the study of leisure, since any methodology used has to overcome the problems of exploring something whose definition and limits are uncertain in relation to women and which is intensely personal as well as being shaped by social structures and processes. Conventional leisure studies approaches have often used survey methods as a major source of data, although it is fair to say that other methods, including more qualitative ones, have also been used. Feminist approaches have tended to use ethnographic methods or interviews much more although as Finch (1985) notes, qualitative research data have not often been used as a basis for social policy changes. But of course surveys do not *necessarily* yield only quantitative data, whilst interviews and ethnographic techniques may well produce data which at some point needs to be quantified (transcripts of people's talk, and interviews, have to be analysed, and there are some moves towards undertaking this by computer). In adddition Graham (1983) notes that

> The wholesale adoption of qualitative research by and for women may thus reinforce the very divisions that feminists are seeking to destroy (p. 136)

. . . by separating the study of women into a marginal cultural world based only on certain kinds of data. On the other hand, survey research, as Graham says, finds it difficult, or impossible, to research precisely those social processes (how gender relations actually work) which influence women's lives and identity, although it is quite good at uncovering the structures of gender relations. Surveys may also blur or fail to uncover those subtle aspects of male–female power relations which are so necessary to any explanation of women's experiences. A number of researchers have emphasized the desirability of using unstructured or semistructured interviews with women and noted the rapport which develops in the course of such interviews (Finch 1984, Oakley 1981) despite the power of the researcher over the subject in contexts where the women being interviewed are underprivileged. Stanley and Wise (1983) emphasize the importance of using our own and other's personal experience in social action and warn against using social science in such a way that it imposes artificially derived frameworks and meanings on reality. Smart (1984) suggests that the job of interviewing is 'intrinsically feminine'. It is certainly the case that whatever method is used, care needs to be taken not to impose meaningless categories on empirical data, but equally it is difficult to see how *any* kind of social analysis is possible without using some kind of categorizing framework. Bowles and Duelli Klein (1983) raise the question of whether a distinguishing feature of research *for* women (as opposed to research *on* women) is the ability to look critically at the methods being used, and assess the extent to which those methods are able to capture the distinctive experiences of women. This could encompass a wide range of methods from diaries and questionnaires to participant observation. Some studies of women's leisure have relied heavily on interviews and participant observation, but other projects (Green, Hebron and Woodward 1985b) have utilized a combination of survey and interview-in-depth techniques which appear to offer both breadth and detailed analysis of a few cases. Diaries are widely used in leisure research of all kinds and have many attractions (lots of data, they appear to be close to women's actual experiences, provide some information about sequence and can give a more fluid picture than a questionnaire or survey interview) but as Wyatt (1985) points out, diaries can yield too much information, not everyone can be relied upon, is literate enough or sufficiently motivated to keep an accurate record of their activities, and diaries often miss out on simultaneous activities or those thought by the diary keeper to be unimportant.

Another major issue concerning methodology is how to get women to talk about leisure when its parameters are so undetermined. Several researchers have found that asking women about the meaning of leisure to them is not as illuminating as might be thought (Green, and Hebron, Green, Hebron and Woodward, 1985b Anderson 1985). Wimbush (1985) points out that using the concept of leisure may invoke masculine connotations of 'free time' and therefore be unhelpful, so that using other terms like well-being may be more thought-provoking. I found in my own research that asking questions about enjoyable and pleasurable aspects of daily routines was sometimes productive, as was getting women to hypothesize about what they would do with a 'free' evening, afternoon or daytime hour. But almost all ways of inquiring about aspects of their lives to which women may give little conscious thought are problematic, because they require women to think in ways which may be quite alien to them. Stanley's (1985) answers to this is to focus on the motivations and experience of the researcher too, and to encourage feedback between the researched and the researcher on how the data is organized and what it represents, particularly since data is rarely used in its entirety but selected out, often by a process which quickly becomes opaque and mysterious. But this may produce a rather abstract interpretation or one which tells us much about the researcher and little about the researched.

So far there has tended to be an assumption that debates about feminist methodology are concerned only with research about women. But as Stanley and Wise (1983) make clear, feminist research cannot *only* be concerned with women, because researching women's oppression also means examining the role of men in that oppression. Indeed, as Smart (1984) notes 'it is equally important for feminists to do research which, while it may concern women, is not necessarily *on* women' (p. 157, italics in original). If men are involved in a feminist research project, then many of the ideas about what might constitute 'good methodological practice' may be less applicable. In particular, as Smart (1984) notes, female researchers are not always more powerful than their subjects. Women interviewing men, especially powerful men, are likely to find this a very different experience from that encountered when interviewing most women. Men, even if not individually powerful, have access to partriarchal modes of manipulating women and are accustomed to using sexism as a weapon to protect their own views and position from women and 'prying' researchers. In the study of leisure this problem of how to 'manage' and extract information from men about their role in enabling or obstructing women's leisure is a massive one, and is no less problematic, in fact possibly more so, when it is women's partners that are being researched rather than leisure providers or powerful decision-makers. This may be one reason, although certainly not the only one, why research focusing on women's leisure has tended to concentrate on women alone. Even this is far from immune from problems relating to men and male manipulation. Anyone who has tried to interview a woman at home for example, will be well aware of how men often 'police' such interviews by popping in and out of the room or by hovering like a bird of prey, attempting to restrict access by researchers to women even when the women concerned are more than happy to participate, or refusing permission altogether. Women themselves will often go to elaborate lengths to prevent husbands or partners from finding out they are being interviewed. Such occurrences are, though extremely irksome, and aggravating, an important part of our data because they provide another indicator of the extent to which women are controlled by men.

But data like this may be missed or not noted down if interviewing is being carried out by market researchers, so that whilst there may be good reasons for using market research agencies, such interviewing needs careful briefing of interviewers and to be supplemented by the researcher herself using other techniques on a smaller group of women. Thus who is doing the research and why are important issues for feminists to consider. Is it, for instance, survey research *per se* which is antithetical to feminist perspectives and purposes or is it survey research which asks the wrong questions in the wrong way and is not sensitive to cues outside of the recorded answers to questions? It would seem to be the latter.

There is little persuasive evidence or argument so far adduced in the debate about feminists methods which convinces me that feminist methodology is about choosing one method rather than another, nor has any one method emerged as distinctively feminist. Furthermore, both qualitative and quantitative data may be useful and necessary; what is crucial is whether the research sees an understanding of women's experience and commitment to changing women's subordinate position in society as major priorities. Pure or 'objective' research which does not seek to change anything cannot be seen as feminist, although it might well be utilized by feminists alongside their own findings. Categorizing and organizing research material does require great sensitivity and the power relations between researcher and researched do need to be taken into account, although it need not be the case that these always operate in favour of the researcher. The debate about methodology is I think well summarized by Smart (1984) who says; 'the idea that there is an ideal type of feminist research is spurious . . . although we may produce principles and ethics for doing research, we may have to recognize that there are as many types of feminist research as there are feminisism' (p. 158).

6. Definitions – many questions but few answers

It may seem rather odd in a book about women and leisure to question the existence of the main concept. But the study of leisure, rather like the study of class, is one that is beset by concerns about definitions and methods, sometimes to the extent that it clouds the intentions of researchers and theorists altogether. Debates about the usefulness and coverage of the concept of leisure however, go far beyond semantics and complex but only-interesting-to-their proponents arguments, since those debates symbolize the history of leisure research and leisure researchers as a largely male preserve, one which has only comparatively recently begun to realize the significance of gender.

The definitional problem about leisure cannot be avoided and indeed there are good reasons not to do so. But at the same time, it is necessary, if one is not to emulate the centipede who started to count its legs but forgot *why* as well as *where* it started, to use the word leisure as though there were a consensus about what it meant, as well as holding open the question of whether existing definitions are the most appropriate in relation to women's lives.

If women are asked directly whether they have any leisure, many will laugh and say 'leisure – what's that – we don't have any!' so not only social scientists are sceptical about whether the concept *is* a meaningful one.

There are however some common elements in definitional efforts, despite the heated debates which go on:

1) Leisure is something (not necessarily an activity) involving choice, not free choice; there are also constraints on that choice (Parry and Johnson 1974; Parker 1981)

2) Leisure is usually pleasurable

3) Leisure can be defined or marked out in relation to other activities such as paid work, life-obligations (eating, sleeping etc.) and activities done non-voluntarily and without pleasure (Parker 1971; McIntosh 1981)

4) Leisure is not necessarily to be found in an activity or time or space themselves, but in the quality of those phenomena or of the person who engaged in it (Parker 1976; Gregory 1982)

5) Leisure may be a social space (Kelly 1981)

6) Leisure may be a period of time (Szalai 1972) clearly demarcated from other periods of time

7) Leisure (for women) is connected to aspects of well-being and health (Wimbush 1985)

although no one definition contains all these elements. As McIntosh (1981) has pointed out, however, the major difficulty with almost all the theoretical work on leisure is that it rarely recognizes the existence of women.

It is not that women's use of 'free time' has been ignored, suggests Roberts (1981), but that 'their feminine perspectives and problems have been rendered invisible' (1981 p. 1). He goes on to suggest that the concept of leisure which sees it as something pursued in free time, does not lend itself very well to the study of women, and proposes that what is needed is a re-examination of the concept of leisure in such a way that women are not excluded. Such a process, Roberts indicates, will involve re-examining male as well as female leisure and exploring the pervasiveness of gender roles. This as Chambers (1985) has noted, is a crucial issue because male notions of time, working hours and work discipline may be fundamentally different from female ideas about time. Stanley (1980) in a much more radical contribution than Roberts, argues further that the problem to be solved is not that of women and leisure but the existing ways of constructing and measuring leisure and work; leisure research has often ignored the practical aspects of leisure (as opposed to the theoretical) especially the constraints of social divisions such as class, race and gender. As Stanley correctly points out, discussion about definitions of leisure is often concluded without any clear rationale for favouring one definition rather than another, although often 'leisure' seems to be what derives from public provision. Stanley put forward the view that it is necessary to look at both leisure and work 'as these are constructed by the experiencing individual or group' (p. 24), since leisure is largely a 'personal' matter. As she says, (p. 24) 'is the woman who is thinking about her career as a physicist while having sex doing "leisure" or "work"? Crucial . . . is intent, meaning or state of mind'.

Gregory (1982) also accepts that leisure is something which refers to quality and meaning (p. 47) 'the importance of leisure lies in what it adds to the quality of the whole life; . . . people's leisure experiences, if they can be compared in qualitative terms: pleasure, fulfilment, satisfaction, recuperation.'

Our discussion of leisure definitions has so far elicited the following further points specifically in relation to women:

1) leisure isn't as easily categorized as many researchers would like us to think
2) meaning is an important aspect of leisure
3) there is a need to avoid dichotomizing *paid* work and leisure as though these were the only essential contrasts
4) where time is fragmented, notions of leisure are likely to differ sharply from where time is compartmentalized. Indeed even the idea that 'spare time' exists is problematic, as Anderson (1985) in her Netherlands research shows. Men faced with a reduction of one hour of paid work are, according to her, much more like to see and define this as extra leisure time than are women.

But even this does not exhaust all the possible problems. There is for example a need to take into account that although all women may share certain experiences in common, they also differ enormously in their social background, interests, ethnic group membership, household composition, economic status, sexual orientation, where they live and whether or not they have children. Green, Hebron and Woodward (1985b) were surprised in the early stages of analysing their survey material to find that far from having too little leisure, some women (single older women for example) had too much. So it is not even as if it were possible to assume that leisure is always a scarce resource of women, even though there are plenty of instances where this is so. It is therefore wise to leave the question of definition here for a while, noting that it involves time, quality, choice within constraints, pleasure and enjoyment, is personally meaningful and is connected to lifestyles and well-being.

7. Do women have leisure?

This initial chapter has really been concerned to air some of the preliminary questions which need to be raised (although it has not necessarily provided answers) in any discussion of women's leisure. These have ranged from the insoluble but crucial question of defining leisure, to why women's leisure is worth studying, and how different the historical 'separation' of work and leisure through industrialization processes appears when seen from women's viewpoint. It has looked briefly at some of the approaches which might be adopted when trying to explain how, where, when and if, leisure slots into women's lives. There has also been a brief delving into the contexts and content of women's leisure, and a discussion about whether there is a distinct feminist methodology. A lot of the questions asked have of necessity been abstract or theoretical ones; almost all of them will be re-examined elsewhere in the book. But there has been an assumption that it *is* possible and worthwhile to study women & leisure.

The next chapter is perhaps a little unusual, in that it deals with a single piece of research done by me in the early 1980s. It does that not because that study (or indeed any other single study) is a 'typical' one, nor because the book is to be based on only one piece of substantive research (which is not the intention). The Milton Keynes study is used because it conveys some of the flavour of researching women's leisure in a particular area, and because it raises many of the issues – leisure and the household, leisure and education, leisure and employment and the politics and provision of leisure facilities – which are the substance of the rest of the book – but does so in a rather more holistic way than is possible in other chapters which are essentially collecting together perspectives and scattered data and findings from a variety of sources about women's leisure.

Hence the next chapter is not intended to be definitive or prescriptive or to provide the basis for wide generalizations, but is offered as a way of beginning to understand why women's leisure is such a complex phenomenon. It is also the beginning of, but very far from the complete answer to the question 'Do women have leisure?' and if so what might it look like?

CHAPTER TWO

Women and leisure in a new town

1. Women and life in Milton Keynes

When I began the research described here in 1980, it was not just an interest in leisure which sparked it off, but rather a wider concern about the lives and employment chances of women in Milton Keynes. Conceived as a new town in an economic boom (it was designated in the late 1960s) and realized in an economic downturn, Milton Keynes displays that contradiction between apparent affluence in public places (huge wide roads for the two-car household, houses with gardens, trees and shrubs everywhere, vast expanses of purpose-built lakes, an enormous covered shopping area) and evident poverty in private places (unemployment rates about the regional average, many single parents struggling to bring up children on low incomes, house interiors whose bleakness belies their bright new external appearance). That is not to say that everyone in Milton Keynes is poor; they are not. For those in well-paid employment, Milton Keynes is an attractive place to live. There are facilities for sport and leisure, a nationally famous (and much visited by non-residents) shopping centre, good road and rail communications (London, Oxford, Cambridge and rural England being within easy reach) and excellent housing for affluent owner-occupiers. But not everyone has found the promised land in Milton Keynes. For some, especially working class women, often moving initially to the city because of the housing opportunities it offered or the employment prospects available (sometimes for their *male* partners rather than themselves) the experience has not lived up to expectations. There is employment in Milton Keynes, some of it very badly paid (Brownfield-Pope, 1985) but there has been a particular problem with women's employment. Many women moving to Milton Keynes have been used to factory or other kinds of semi or unskilled work, but there is little such employment available in the city. Secretarial, clerical, retail selling, cleaning and catering offer the major employment opportunities for women without advanced educational or professional qualifications. Consequently many women who might otherwise be in full-time employment are either unemployed or in part-time jobs. It was really concern about the experiences of such women (and others) in Milton Keynes which precipitated my study.

Other features of Milton Keynes relevant to leisure are the skewed age structure, (the population of the city is younger than the country as a whole, with many adult residents in their twenties and thirties) and the co-existence of newly built estates with more established urban and village settlements. The latter are more likely to have private, commercial leisure provision, whereas the new city is dominated by public leisure provision, and commercial leisure resources are only just beginning to emerge on a large scale. The population was around 120,000 in 1985, of whom about one-third had moved to the city from London. There are no high rise flats in the newly constructed areas, and although low-rise flats are available these are occupied in the main by single people. Larger households are much more likely to live in a house or bungalow with a garden; 49 per cent of householders in 1983 were owner-occupiers. The city is organized on a grid-square road pattern, each grid square containing a housing development, usually but not always accompanied by a small local shopping centre and a public house; some estates have their own purpose-built meeting places. Because of the predominance of young adults, the birth rate is high, and new schools are still (1985) being opened for the large numbers of children and teenagers living in the city. As with all new towns there is administrative overlap between a non-elected Development Corporation and the local (in this case Borough) Council. Milton Keynes is located also in the shire county of Buckinghamshire, a county which is traditionally run by a Conservative administration, and into which Milton Keynes fits somewhat oddly, being very different in character and social class composition from the leafy affluent villages and small towns of the South Bucks commuter belt.

A recent (1983) city-wide survey of household found that some 80 per cent of the sample were happy living in Milton Keynes, mostly for reasons related to the environment, including access to parks and countryside, shopping facilities, the road system and car-parking facilities (no multi-storey car parks). Dislikes were most to do with social facilities– the lack of night life, difficulties in meeting people and making friends, and the absence of an ice rink, any cinema showing major films (this has now been rectified), ten-pin bowling and theatre. Nearly two-thirds felt sports facilities to be satisfactory (*Executive Lifestyle*, 1985) although these are mostly concentrated in leisure centres and in a small number of areas rather than each estate having its own and there are almost no facilities for athletes. On the whole it is the absence of commercial rather than public facilities which residents miss most. A former chief architect and planner Derek Walker, commenting on planned and current leisure provision in Milton Keynes said 'In the city centre we have lost... the chance to look at leisure in a more interesting and original way. Discos, bingo clubs and a cinema complex is not what I would call leisure for a place like Milton Keynes. For its size there is not enough for people to do yet... there is still a massive need for a central centre for arts and leisure activity' (Walker, 1985, p. 12). But of course the focus on leisure in all these discussions, whether favourable or critical, is on out-of-home activities which in the main cost money and require transport and time. For many unwaged women and others living on low incomes, and with myriad household obligations, such debates bear little relevance to their own opportunities for leisure. As we shall see later, there is a sharp division between those women in the city heavily engaged in out-of-home leisure and those for whom leisure occurs largely within the confines of the home. But for both groups, and for those whose experiences are somewhat in-between the two, living in a new city is an important factor shaping their lives. Milton Keynes is not in any sense 'typical' even of other new towns, and certainly not of established cities in the British Isles. But nevertheless, what happens to women there does capture some of the important elements of being a woman in the 1980s.

What follows is an attempt to explore some of the dimensions of women's leisure, and their lives as a whole, in a community context, because it is, as I discovered, very difficult to research women's leisure without simultaneously engaging in an analysis of their lives as a whole, men's relationships to and power over women, and a community study.

2. The Milton Keynes case-study

The research was mostly carried out in the period 1980–1982, and was based on a number of different methods, one (questionnaires) rather unsatisfactory but necessary because of time and financial constraints on the project. The methods included questionnaires (postal and personally handed-out), in-depth semi-structured interviews, discussion groups with local women, meetings with leisure-providers, and observation (both participant and non-participant) of local groups, clubs and activities as well as communities. Overall, the project involved 497 women living either in the designated area of the city of Milton Keynes or within the boundaries of the Borough of

Milton Keynes (a geographical area larger than the city itself). There were two main stages in the research. The first stage (known hereafter as Study A) took place in 1980–81 and involved looking at what was hypothesized to be an atypical group–women with leisure pursuits or interests *outside* the home. These ranged from women using leisure centres, attending evening classes or bingo sessions, and members of sports or hobby clubs, to women who belonged to branches of local or national women's organizations (for example the National Housewives Register, Women's Institutes or groups of women living on the same estate and meeting regularly). Some 329 women were involved at this stage of the project. Questionnaires were used as one major source of data, being handed to women encountered at different locations, from leisure centre foyers to flower arranging clubs and bingo sessions, with some completed forms being returned by post (sealed, addressed envelopes were provided); others were given back to me depending on the location and time available. There was a response rate of 54 per cent for these questionnaires (195/361 returned). A further 134 women either participated in group discussions with me or were interviewed individually (once, sometimes twice) using a semi-structured schedule. The second phase of the study (hereafter referred to as Study B) involved looking at a random sample of women from five different areas of Milton Keynes, and occurred in 1981 and 1982. A combination of questionnaires and interviews was again used. The response rate on the questionnaires was slightly lower than in the first phase (51 per cent–168 returned from 330) but it was rather more detailed than that used in stage one, and was sent through the post rather than being presented personally by the researcher. Thirty unstructured interviews with women were carried out after these questionnaires were returned. The women selected for interview were chosen both for geographical location in different city areas and because their questionnaires indicated that they represented a cross-section of the women in the second stage of the research. This second stage (Study B) was intended to discover what a randomly selected group of women thought about their lives, including work, leisure and education, and was deliberately chosen as a contrast to the 'women involved-in-leisure-out-of-the home' phase of the project.

The research aroused a lot of local interest amongst groups and women's organizations not involved in it directly, and so it was possible to talk through some of the findings not only with some of those who had participated, but also with local women who had not, an important methodological and political point. As someone closely involved in local politics since 1981, I hope I have also been able to feed back some of the results into local authority and other decision-making processes too. As a feminist I feel strongly that although much research is inevitably constructed more from the viewpoint of the research, and/or research sponsor, it is important that women actually gain something from the research and are able to look at, and respond to, the findings. So for instance I did revisit some groups of women who had been involved in the first stage of the study once I had analysed the results of that and sent copies of the paper to others. Very few women were unwilling to talk to me. I had only two refusals on individual interviews and one from a group of women – but there were understandably many reasons for non-return of questionnaires, including illness, mislaid questionnaires, holidays and lack of time, and some I did not discover at all. One or two women were angry about being asked questions relating to who did housework in their household, and three felt it to be an invasion of their privacy to be asked to fill in a questionnaire. What I had not expected (although perhaps on reflection I should have) was letters from husbands and male co-habitees telling me that their wives/partners were not going to be allowed to complete my questionnaire. So wrote one man; 'I write to say my wife won't be filling your form in – what a cheek – her time is *my* business' (my italics). This was despite taking elaborate steps to ensure the anonymity of those returning questionnaires and asking no direct questions on the form (I *did* ask in interviews) about money. In itself this response from males is indicative of the attitudes some men had towards 'their' women and was a useful, if rather disturbing, source of data, as were the difficulties sometimes experienced in arranging times and places to interview women in their homes undisturbed by a male presence.

3. Women outside the home – active pursuit of leisure?

The first stage of the Milton Keynes (Study A) research began with contacting all the organizations, clubs and societies in the city which had women members. It then involved distributing questionnaires to 361 women using out-of-home leisure facilities, belonging to various organizations or otherwise engaged in out-of-home leisure; this was far from an ideal method, and the response rate (195 returned from 361) was about as high as anticipated. But in itself this part of the research was useful for the insights it offered into where women were to be found outside the home and the range of activities offered. I also talked to the local authority, Development Corporation and a small number of commercial leisure planners and providers about what was available locally to women and future developments. Subsequently I visited and observed many women's and mixed organizations and clubs, and held group discussions with members. I also conducted a small number of individual interviews with users of leisure facilities.

I knew when I first considered doing research on leisure in this way that the women I would be observing, talking to and asking to complete questionnaires were not in any sense typical, because national surveys suggest that only certain groups and ages of women are involved in leisure outside the home. I was aware too that I was unable to cover all the possibilities – work groups at lunch-time for example, or discos – and that my methods were not necessarily the best combination for the purpose. Nevertheless, the combination of questionnaires, observations, discussions and interviews yielded some useful data about what women can do outside the home and which women are most likely to be involved. I also learnt a great deal about the situation of women who had recently moved to live in new towns; 'well I do like it – but I miss my mum – and my friends – it's lonely sometimes' said one woman I met with her son at a leisure centre. There were also some interesting points about the role played by women living in more established residential centres on the periphery of the new city, some of whom regretted the city as did this locally-born woman 'it's spoilt it, really – too many people, too much noise, too much traffic'. The findings in this part of the study were particularly revealing because whilst showing that some women do have the time and space for leisure in their lives, they also made evident some of the constraints within which such leisure operates and demonstrated the complex interweaving of leisure with other aspects of women's lives. In particular data indicated that there is often a blurred line between unpaid work and leisure, but a clearer demarcation between paid work and leisure. It also taught me not to jump to rapid conclusions about what women might gain from particular activities or interests; it is frequently not as obvious as one might think. The research findings also show that women, far from disliking the company of other women, actually seek it out. The study made clear the very marginal role which sport plays in the lives of most women, although obviously many factors affect this, from age and physical infirmity to dependent children (Chapter Four discusses this in more detail).

i. What makes out-of-home leisure possible; what does it comprise?

Studying women whose leisure time and interests are pursued at least partially outside the home, helps make apparent not only the different situations women may find themselves in, but also the range of activities and interests which women's out-of-home leisure may encompass. There were many activities which didn't receive the indepth study they needed, but others were seen in a new light – community and voluntary organizations, for example and flower-arranging clubs. It was also very instructive in this first phase of the study to talk to both male and female policy makers and leisure providers. The former mostly couldn't understand why few or no women joined in their particular activity or interest. A chess club secretary plaintively asked me to tell him why his club attracted no women; 'As you seem to be an expert, please write and tell me your results', and the secretary of a cycling club said they couldn't make cycling any easier but there were still few women members. Female policy-makers and those involved with providing leisure (mostly non-commercial) had a much better idea of where women's interests lie and why they might not get involved with things at certain points. Women connected with leisure provision were also more likely to appreciate the social and economic situation and sheer isolation of the many Milton Keynes women newly or recently arrived in the city, often without a job, and not near relatives or friends.

ii. Influences on leisure

A number of crucial factors, apart from gender, merge from the first phase of the research as major determinants of the leisure experiences of women outside the home – social class, age, life cycle stage, friendship and employment status. Other factors which are very important – ethnicity, for example – didn't emerge strongly because there were not enough women from ethnic minority groups in the sample (this reflects both who lives in Milton Keynes and which women are active outside the home). Most other factors were dependent on those already outlined, for example being able to drive. Other factors – fear of walking alone on Milton Keynes footpaths/cycleway system, or fears about sexual harassment in public places – were common to all women, whether heavily involved in out-of-home leisure or not, and were shared constraints which in themselves didn't explain which women were active in out-of-home leisure and which were less so. So for instance children of many ages, including over seventeens, were a barrier for some but not all women. Some women had the support of their families or household members in their activities, others did not but continued anyway. Involvement in leisure out-of-home was sometimes traded off against a job; for instance a husband might be happy for his wife to belong to a flower arranging club and go to bingo with her friends, but less happy if she took a part-time job involving no more hours out of the house. Others found that having a job was a reason for husbands restricting them 'you're out too often now' but was also a better lever than housework for arguing back. Leisure, over the lifetime of an individual, is never static, and changes in response not only to alterations in life cycle and economic circumstance, but also geographical and social mobility. What was possible or enjoyable in London or Birmingham is not necessarily either possible or enjoyable in Milton Keynes; 'I often used to get on the bus and go to the West End–just window shopping. I can't go now–not here–it's not the same'. Similarly the activities or interests engaged in by working-class teenage girls may give way to others not just because of age, but also because having a more middle-class life style as a thirty year old adult changes attitudes and tastes. 'Dancing, that used to be my thing–afraid its bingo now'.

iii. Who does what?

Part of this stage of the research involved looking at who used what leisure facilities or belong to which groups. I found three distinct patterns. First there were those places–bingo sessions, leisure centres, swimming pools, community workshops, adult education classes, keep fit and yoga and dance sessions, tennis clubs, W.I. branches for example–where women went on their own or with other women; such places were generally used only or mainly by women (or at least this was so at particular times of the day or week) and this was one major reason for the popularity of such activities and locations. Another reason for popularity was that women had chosen to go themselves because they enjoyed the activities.

Secondly there were activities and locations involving children– including walking, swimming, visits to local parks or lakes, leisure centre visits and matinee sessions at cinemas. Sometimes the activities were genuinely shared ones–picnicking by Willen lake, or swimming. But on many other occasions women were present mainly to accompany or chauffeur their offspring, and whilst they might enjoy just sitting quietly waiting for a child at a gym or Judo class, or talking to other waiting mothers, these latter purposes were not the main reason for their being in a particular place. This does not of course mean that no pleasure was derived from the activity or location, but it does mean that women's choice in most contexts was very limited–the real choice often lay with children.

Thirdly there were activities and locations involving women and men, mainly, but not exclusively in male–female couples. Included in this third category were pubs, restaurants, cinemas and concerts and some sports facilities–of course the categories were not absolute, and sometimes I found married couples who went to bingo sessions together, or women who went to pubs or for meals out with other women.

iv. Locations and times for leisure

Location and activity did have an important effect on who went where, why, and with whom (if anyone) they went. So too did the time of day, and whether or not it was dark. So in early September at 7pm I found far more women out in Milton Keynes than in December as the same time when it was dark. At night generally women alone or with other women were to be found only in places or activities which they regarded as relatively 'safe' (evening classes, clubs, keep fit sessions and bingo rather than the cinema, or pubs). These were also regarded by male partners as 'unthreatening', but the reasons were different—women felt safe (i.e. from sexual harassment, assault or rape) when they were with other women. In a place where men, if present, were also themselves engaged in some kind of specific activity (for example evening classes) then women also felt safer than if simply 'out', drinking, walking or sitting. Men also apparently felt happier about 'their' women being out where they would not encounter other men—but this was often motivated as much or more by jealousy and their concern to control their female partners' sexuality, or to exercise control over their lives, as by concerns about threats of violence or harassment.

v. Class and age

I expected that age and social class would play a part in which women were active outside the home, and this did prove to be the case. Young women in their late teens and early twenties, and women in their forties and fifties were the most visible. Women in their late twenties or in their thirties, especially those with dependent children were least likely to be found involved in leisure outside the home, although social class factors also played a part here. [It is of course notoriously difficult to define women's social class. Here their present and/or last occupations were used.] Middle class women in professional jobs for instance, even in the late twenties to thirties age group and with dependent children, were to be found at adult education classes, in the WI or Inner Wheel, at leisure centres and so on. Working class women of a similar age and at a similar stage in their life cycle were by no means absent from *all* out-of-home activities—walking with their children for example, or going to leisure centres or joining in some women's organizations (house-wives groups on various estates for example, or the WI) but they were much less evident as a group than their younger or older peers. Some working class women had particular difficulties—husbands on low pay working long shifts, or being employed away from home, although the latter had its compensations; 'When he's at home I can't do anything – he needs feeding or attention all the time. When he's working away, as long as I take the kids, I can please myself' (woman met at community workshop). But it should not be thought that working class women were the only ones to experience problems with their leisure. During an illuminating discussion with an Inner Wheel (an organization for wives of Rotarians) group, we got onto the subject of entertaining – one member said

> We entertain a lot – I used to enjoy it – but I'm not so sure now . . . (why's that?)
> Well we used to invite friends, people we both liked, but now it tends to be my husband's business associates. So I have to take a lot of time planning what to cook, and buying the right kinds of foodstuffs . . . then I worry about what I'm wearing . . . what to say . . . will the cooking turn out well. It's hardly relaxing. I'd never thought about it before – my husband says I should enjoy entertaining. I think he *does* . . . but he only has to serve the drinks . . . it's me that's on show . . . so it's hardly my leisure, is it?

vi. *Employment and leisure*

Being in employment was another striking feature of those women, of whatever age, who were involved in out-of-home leisure. Women's employment is notorious for its low level of wages, so that it wasn't necessarily financial independence which made the crucial difference (although having your own money, however tiny the amount, can't be underestimated), but rather the extent to which having a part-time or full-time job allowed women to be legitimately outside their homes, even if husbands complained that their wives were never in. 'He doesn't like it much – but once I'm out he can't really fetch me home – we often go for a quick drink when we've all finished at 7.30' (Cleaner). Employment also seemed to provide a source of women friends, status and a degree of confidence about being in control of life. Jobs also structure time, so that leisure becomes possible as an exclusive activity rather than as one activity carried out simultaneously with others. There were some affluent middle class women without employment who were very active outside the home, but they were involved in the main, in a very distinct group of leisure interests and pursuits, for example voluntary work through the Inner Wheel or Ladies Circle, or daytime badminton classes or riding lessons. There were also some working class women without jobs to be found too, in some cases searching hard for jobs, (and hence involved in adult or further education classes for vocational rather than leisure reasons) but also to be found at bingo sessions, keep fit and a small range of other activities or interests.

Generally, working class women seemed to 'prefer' activities they could do on a casual basis, rather than needing to plan ahead or set aside particular times each week – there were often financial reasons for this as well as the unpredictability of domestic routine which could disrupt leisure unexpectedly.

vii. Enjoyable out-of-home leisure

The main activities and interests enjoyed by Milton Keynes women in Study A fall into a number of categories, some overlapping:

1) relatively unorganized interests/activities – meeting friends for a gossip, going out for a walk, sunbathing by one of the area's many lakes, going for a drink (most women).

2) sports – some 60 per cent of the women involved in some kind of sport (this is extremely high compared to national surveys but partly reflects the way data was collected), with swimming, badminton, yoga and keep fit as the most popular. Most sports were engaged in outside of clubs and were, apart from badminton, tennis and squash, entirely non-competitive.

3) commercial leisure/entertainments – bingo (sometimes run by local groups) pubs, discos, cinema, concerts, theatre productions (about two thirds of all women in the sample)

4) publicly provided leisure – leisure centres, sports facilities, evening and day adult education classes, libraries, cycleways, footpaths etc. (about two thirds of all the women, but adult education is probably over-represented because of the way data was collected).

5) hobby/special interests organizations – including flower arranging, tennis, church, music, pressure groups and political parties (about 30 per cent).

6) women's organizations – ranging from mothers' clubs to the W.I., and from those purely concerned with their members interests (e.g. National Housewives Register) to those who play a major role in community, charitable and or fund-raising activities (Inner Wheel, Business and Professional Women's Clubs etc.) (about 23 per cent).

Despite this wide range of activities, the questionnaires, group discussions and individual interviews used revealed a number of problems which women experienced in relation to leisure. These included male attitudes towards women going out alone or with friends – many husbands or partners were only happy if the activity was approved of by them (keep fit was; discos or the pub usually weren't) and the hours of employment or other commitments of partners were appropriate. Childcare (or alternative chauffering/ accompanying arrangements for older children) was a problem for some. But there were fewer mothers of young children in this phase of the research than the Milton Keynes population structure would suggest is typical. Housework and domestic obligations were a problem for all except single women living alone. Women without access to private transport found evening activities and those located at some distance from their homes difficult, but in this aspect of the research under a third of women were in that category (this reflects the 'self-selected' nature of the sample). Lack of money and absence of close friends living nearby were also significant factors for a minority.

viii. Communities and leisure; the new and the old

The research also revealed some interesting findings about leisure and rootedness in a community. Although Milton Keynes is a new city with a still-increasing population, many of the women I encountered during the research were long-established residents or geographically mobile middle-class women rather than those who had moved significant distances (that is to Milton Keynes) only once in their lives. Indeed many of the more organized women's activities took place largely outside the newer areas of the city, where meeting places were cheaper to hire and community networks already set up. Such activities thus involved either established residents, women from villages outside the city or middle class professional women used to moving from one town to another. Certain women emerged as key figures in facilitating and arranging the leisure of others. For instance, I found the same woman (of long standing residence) leading a walk with the Rambling Club, closely involved with a local W.I. Branch, running a handicrafts evening class and heavily committed to various charitable groups too. In her 'spare' time this woman also ran an allotment, had three school-age children and gave talks to local schools about domestic crafts. In a newly established community such people are rare; comparable skills and networks of contacts take time to develop. One common feature of new areas in Milton Keynes is the rapid appearance and demise of groups and activities, as those responsible for their formation lose interest or move away. Other out-of-home activities did not attract the number of recently arrived women that they might for a whole variety of reasons – insecurity, and lack of confidence, no friends, no money (no job or/and the expense of moving and furnishing a new home).

ix. Study A – a summary

The first stage of the project then, concerned itself with women who are not, according to existing surveys and research, typical in either their leisure concerns or their determination to be involved in out-of-home leisure. But at the same time such a study is able to uncover some of the constraints which affect women's leisure – from social class and money, to dual home and employment roles and the need to facilitate children's leisure or accommodate husbands' 'time-off' and hours of work. In addition, but very importantly it demonstrates the extent to which the public world to which women have access is a very different and much more restricted world than that to which men have access, for reasons which are very much connected to the individual and collective power men wield over women. As one woman whom I met at a W.I. branch meeting said when I asked her if her husband minded her being a W.I. member

> No – not really – he thinks I won't get up to any mischief while I'm here – mind I have to leave everything just so . . . meal ready to eat when he comes in . . . house tidy . . . kids doing their homework upstairs . . . or its murder when I get back . . . when *he* goes to the pub *he* never asks me if *I* can manage while he's out – it just wouldn't occur to him.

Single women in employment (though not usually single mothers, who had problems with childcare, money and sometimes social isolation), who in many ways might be thought of as having an ideal situation for leisure, had many more activities or interests than most women who lived in larger households, but were also influenced by where it was appropriate for them to be seen. 'There are some pubs I'd never go in, even with a woman friend – blokes just stare at you all the time, or come up and ask you to go out with them. It doesn't occur to them you might just want a drink.' (single woman in her twenties).

4. Leisure at home – Study B

The second phase of the research concentrated on a random sample, with the expectations that most women would be involved principally in in-home activities rather than out-of-home ones. The difficulties that women experience in being part of the public world which men take for granted might lead us to suppose that the ideal is leisure in the home, which is theoretically available to all. It requires less money, less time, and is, it might be supposed, hinged about with fewer constraints. Interestingly the 'out-of-home leisure' sample were also extremely involved in home-based leisure too, with TV, sewing, knitting and gardening being favourites.

i. What is at-home leisure?

At-home leisure also presents problems, both in terms of who, what and when, but also in relation to the difficulties many women experience in separating out time and space (physical as well as mental) for themselves. Furthermore the dividing line between public and private worlds, or between in-home and out-of-home is by no means as clear-cut as it might appear. As well as spending a great deal of time in their own homes, women may also spend much time in the homes, of friends and/or relatives, for a variety of purposes ranging from duty visits to in-laws to shared leisure times spent talking, or eating. Amongst women without employment, home selling of various kinds (clothes, cosmetics, children's books) may be a source of income, social contact and enjoyment which is mostly conducted in the home of others, and so is located in a semi-public, semi-private world. There is not only a definitional problem about what counts as in-home leisure but a methodological one too. Whilst interviewing can be and was done in women's homes, and questionnaires can and did ask about in-home leisure, the role of participant and non-participant observation in relation to home leisure is strictly limited, whereas in Study A these were important sources of information.

There is also another area of difficulty concerning at-home leisure. Whilst the problems of defining women's leisure are immense anyway, home-based leisure is if anything harder to determine that out-of-home leisure, since it is even more likely to overlap with, or occur concurrently with non-leisure activities. So for instance, activities such as knitting, sewing, gardening and cooking were extremely popular leisure activities and seen as enjoyable but *only under certain conditions.* So, gardening is enjoyable when it involves creating a rock-garden or tending well-loved plants on a sunny day with a whole afternoon available, but not when it means taming an overgrown lawn on an overcast evening as well as cooking tea, washing three machine-loads of clothes, cleaning the kitchen and bathing children. Knitting and sewing may be undertaken as a way of saving expenditure on clothes *or* as an activity which is itself enjoyable *and* can be done whilst talking, watching TV or in odd moments of time snatched from the daily routine. Cooking may be an unenviable time-consuming, monotonous and frustrating task for much of the week, month or year, but some women derive great enjoyment from baking cakes and bread, even if the end result meets with no more enthusiasm from consumers than a 'meat and two veg' evening meal. Similarly cooking a special meal for friends can be enjoyable, whilst entertaining relatives or business/work acquaintances may not be.

ii. *Contrasts between Studies A and B*

Differences between the women encountered during phase A of the research and those in phase B related not just to variations in activities undertaken but to the characteristics of the women themselves. The women in sample A included many middle class women, women in full-time employment, without young children, women able to drive and with access to a car, and women who had experienced an extended education. In age terms, the phase A sample comprised mainly women under thirty and those over forty-five. The random sample (B) whilst not quite the polar opposite (because it did contain a few women with the above characteristics) contained many working class women in the thirty to forty-five age group with dependent children under seventeen, over half of whom were not currently in employment, (although a quarter were in full-time jobs). Many had left school at the minimum leaving age and only a minority held a full driving licence. Clubs, organizations and groups of various kinds played a much less important role in these women's lives, and the numbers involved in any variety of sport of physical activity were very low. Nearly a quarter of the sample lived in households where at least one adult was unemployed (the unemployment rate in Milton Keynes is above the S.E. region average). Whereas in Study A, most women had been on holiday during the twelve months preceding the study, in Study B there was a significant minority who had not had a holiday in the last year, and others whose holidays consisted of day trips, or staying with relatives.

iii. *Entitlement to leisure*

One of the most striking differences in the two groups was their view of leisure and leisure entitlement. Whilst women in Study A saw leisure activities, enjoyment and pleasure as important parts of their lives and actively tried to ensure that their routines and lifestyles included these things, women in Study B, whilst not seeing their lives as devoid of interest or enjoyment, derived their enjoyment, pleasure and relaxation mostly from their domestic situations, rather than from activities or interests specifically undertaken because they were different from or in separate contexts from normal domestic routine. This difference between the two groups was at its most acute for those women without employment in Study B. It was such women who either saw themselves as having no 'right' to leisure or who felt they had no time and too many conflicting obligations, to do things which contributed only to their *own* enjoyment or relaxation (anything which was also for others' enjoyment, for example children and/or partners, was seen differently). As one woman said

> Of course there are things I'd like to do – I'd like to go jogging, go to the cinema, go out for the day somewhere without the others . . . but I feel it's too selfish, I'd be neglecting the children . . . and the house . . . they come first.

Women in employment in both samples were much better able both to compartmentalize their time and to assert their need for time and space for themselves, regardless of their other commitments.

iv. *Constraints on leisure*

If we look at home-based activities of the two groups A and B, there does not at first seem to be much difference. TV, sitting down, reading and gardening are popular with both, but there are fewer crafts done by group B, and the overall range of interests with children also figures much more strongly for women in group B, which is only partly a reflection of the characteristics of the second group. Many more than in group A find some aspects of housework enjoyable, and care of children takes up more time (partly because these are, on the whole, younger children). The 'social lives' of group B are perceived to be more frequently interrupted by their domestic and childcare obligations, partner's job and leisure interests, than group A, although it is fair to say that there are also problems faced by the first group. The difference is that whilst women in Sample A have found ways of overcoming these constraints, women in Sample B haven't generally been able to do this: a typical example of the latter is as follows;

> My friend says I ought to get out more . . . but I get so tired . . . even when I haven't got anything much else to do, I don't feel like going out, and I know Jim (husband) wouldn't like it, and the kids hate it if I'm off somewhere without them, even if they go to Joyce's (aunt) which they like doing.

There are a lot of complex factors at work here – confidence, status personal inclination, feelings of well-being and degree of support from others in the household, as well as household obligations which can all influence whether women turn to at home or out-of-home activities as a means of relaxation and enjoyment.

v. *Actual and desired leisure*

Study B women differ not only in their social background, class membership and domestic situations, but also in the gap between what they actually do and what they would like to do. Whilst sample A were by no means all happily engaged in all the activities and interests they wanted, (indeed as women get older and go through different stages of the life cycle, what they want to do and are able to do, changes anyway), group B were much more likely either to hanker after pursuits they'd previously enjoyed or feel that there were many things they'd like to do, but couldn't. These things ranged from going dancing to learning to windsurf. The reasons stopping them were many – no money, no time, partner's disapproval, no transport, anxiety, not knowing how/where to go or who to ask, domestic responsibilities – and were not always different to the problems faced by the first group (who also sometimes wanted to do things they weren't able to engage in currently). But group B were much less able to overcome these, or felt that, as many said; 'well, I'll just have to wait until the children are older'. Others said they'd change when they moved; thinking about and actually moving house is a major preoccupation in Milton Keynes, not to another town but to elsewhere within the city itself – this is encouraged by the variety of new private housing available to buy but is also not uncommon in the public sector too. In a few cases, waiting until they got divorced was a constraint.

Something more immediate – TV, writing letters, gardening, knitting or taking a nap was always easier to arrange, and the times and spaces themselves often sufficiently erratic or unpredictable enough to ensure that nothing major (joining an organization, enrolling in a class, learning a new skill etc.) could be undertaken, even if other constraints like no money or lack of transport were removed. Asked what they would do with a free day, most women in Study B, apart from seeing such a thing as a fantasy, opted for shopping (this was not, as they all emphatically said, for *food*) going on an outing, sleeping late, and visiting friends rather than the wide range of activities women in sample A were already engaged in, or the kind of things that women in study B themselves thought they might like to do but saw as unavailable. That is, the choices amongst women in study B made within a range of things they thought were possible *given their present situation and constraints*. Only in relation to what they'd like to do on holiday (not necessarily what they *actually* did as not all of them had holidays) did any sense of activities outside their present experience and lives emerge, perhaps because holidays are seen as times when some lifting of constraints is possible. Somewhat ironically, actual holidays for many working class women consist of the same domestic routine as usual but under the more cramped conditions of tent, static caravan or rented flat.

vi. Comparisons of out-of-home leisure

The out-of-home activities of Study B women were much more limited in their extent than those of group A. Organizations, sport and evening classes were all of minor significance, although they were more prominent for women in employment and for single women. Popular were walking, seeing friends, and going out with partners for a drink or meal; single women and a few over-fifties were also likely to include dancing. Enjoyment and pleasure were derived from aspects of daily routine including children, and meeting friends. Women in study B with jobs said that they got a particular satisfaction from knowing that they had finished their jobs for the day, and that whilst domestic obligations awaited them, they could also relax, *or* felt that their job was in itself a source of enjoyment. This latter referred not just to the content of the job (many jobs were indeed not particularly enjoyable ones), but to the sociability of working with other people and to having their own money. Although some women in study B without paid employment said they gained satisfaction and enjoyment from their work at home, the enjoyment was unrelated to money (they seldom had any of their own) and rarely referred to sociability (since isolation at home was a frequent complaint). Activities with partners for those women not living alone or with children were quite popular in the group amongst both samples A and B, but were more likely to be domestically-based, or focused around going out for a drink or a meal for group B than women in study A, who more often were involved in shared sporting, educational or organizational activities together.

vii. Friendship

Friendship is an important aspect of women's leisure and enjoyment, and this is a particular problem in a new town, especially for working class women who are (on the whole) less used to moving to new areas than the more socially and geographically mobile middle classes. Whereas in sample A out-of-home and at-home activities were frequently shared with friends of the same sex (as opposed to men, or couples) this was less common amongst women in sample B. Not only this, but sample B were less likely to have all their close friends living nearby (sometimes they had not yet made any new friends as opposed to casual acquaintances since moving to the city), and less likely also to have female relatives (mothers, aunts, sisters) living near them. So the sources of female support and companionship were often limited. This can and does affect not only willingness to be involved in out-of-home activities for the first time, but also women's confidence to assert the right to time for themselves, their feelings of vulnerability whilst walking or travelling across the city, and the places that they feel able to go to (a pub or cinema is likely to be somewhere an unaccompanied woman won't visit, whereas with a friend it may be possible).

5. Reflections on leisure in Milton Keynes

The main differences between the two samples then relate not only to variations in socio-economic background and age, but also the activities undertaken, where these take place, the extent to which unshared or 'selfish' leisure is seen as legitimate, and the ease or difficulty with which constraints on leisure are met or overcome. But it is easy to exaggerate the differences between the two groups, or overestimate its importance; there *are* similarities, and to the extent that the two differ it is often a question of degree rather than *absolute* difference. Both groups have problems and constraints which it is necessary for them to overcome if they are to have any leisure of their own. Whilst some of those constraints and problems are of necessity individual and idiosyncratic, many of them are both structural and ideological and there is a limit to which individual women can challenge such constraints. Some women, as we have seen from study A and from the employed women in study B, are better at meeting such challenges than others. More often than not this is because they possess certain social and economic advantages, ranging from educational or occupational qualifications, full-time employment and the absence of dependent (or at any rate very young) children, to social status, confidence and car ownership.

Even women who are able to challenge or resist some of the constraints surrounding the possibilities of achieving leisure outside the home and inside it, are limited by the extent to which male dominance permeates society. Whether it is the difficulties women face in being able to escape from the household tasks in the evenings or weekends, the places and activities with which they feel comfortable, vulnerability when travelling across a city, or the extent to which women are made to feel that sport and physical activity are unfeminine, it is male dominance, in its many forms which stands at the roots of these constraints. This isn't to say that there are no other determinants–it isn't simply male dominance, but capitalist modes of production too which condemn many women to free domestic labour and undervalued underpaid employment–but merely to point out that women are not free agents in 'choosing' what to do in their leisure. Their leisure, whatever its extent or absence, is significantly controlled and influenced by men. Even amongst women who felt no sense of resentment about this, there was in the research an awareness that most men were able to enjoy leisure in a much more unfettered way than most women. Men see themselves as having a right to leisure, most women do not. But furthermore men see the public world as theirs. Women are tolerated in some parts of it or in certain capacities (it is possible for women to serve behind bars where the presence of a lone woman or two women drinking would not be tolerated) but not in others. There are few equivalent spaces and places barred to men to which they might otherwise want to go.

Where women are active in leisure pursuits outside the home it is usually within a range of 'suitable' and 'gender appropriate' activities – women's organizations, caring and community activities, evening classes, keep fit and yoga groups, bingo, which are enjoyable, but are also where women feel and are perceived by men to be 'safe' and 'women in their place'. This is however in no sense to denigrate the value of the activities women do, because many of them are immensely important in helping women acquire the confidence, skills, and knowledge of the world which so many men take for granted. But the 'choices' women have are extremely restricted, and male dominance is a powerful element in retaining that restriction.

6 Four women and their leisure

I want to end this chapter by looking at four women who were amongst the many that I talked to and interviewed, and who illustrate some of the different strands and experiences of leisure which have been discussed hitherto.

(1) Mrs A

Mrs A lives in an established area of the city, in a well-furnished semi-detached privately owned house. She is in her early thirties and has a three year old daughter. Prior to her daughter's birth she had a well-paid administrative job with a large company, a job she enjoyed. She left school at 18 with 'A' levels and did a college course afterwards. She now has a part-time job – selling children's books at parties – 'because your brain goes stale when you're at home all the time' and because 'we need the money'. But otherwise she enjoys being at home with her child, from whom she derives much pleasure, because she feels she has more freedom to choose her own interests and follow her own inclinations. Her husband is in a professional job, and plays rugby at weekends. Otherwise much of their leisure is shared – DIY, going out for a drink or meal when they can afford it, walks in the countryside nearby, watching TV, playing with their daughter. Her husband does help with housework although 'as I'm here all the time I do more – he hasn't much time really'. He is happy to stay in when Mrs A goes off to sell her books or when she attends her evening classes. She always enrols in at least one a year, it was two or three when she had a full-time job – macrame, crochet, hostess and other specialized cookery classes – being some of the topics she's enjoyed. In addition she visits an old-age pensioner each week (she got in touch with her through a local volunteer bureau) to talk and do odd jobs for her. She has plenty of friends, mostly women with young children who she's met through the local play group or through a local group of mothers who meet once a month, and couples who she and her husband invite round to their house for meals, although she finds her immediate neighbours rather unfriendly. Mrs A feels quite content with her life, and can't think of anything much (other than more money!) that she'd like to be able to do.

(2) Ms B.

Ms B lives in a Development Corporation flat near the city centre which she shares with another woman. She is 26 and a secretary/ personal assistant with a large company. She left school at 16 with 6 'O' levels. She has no children and has never been married (although she has a boyfriend) and has her own car. She is ambitious in her job (she has 2 'A' levels as well as secretarial qualifications all of which she acquired at evening classes), and wants to move on to more executive-type work sooner or later, but she is also very interested in preserving her leisure time. She says 'I have a lively social life – I am rarely in more than one night a week' and neither she nor her flat mate spend much time on housework 'except if we've got visitors – especially my mother' and they mostly eat out or live on snacks. Ms B is very keen on sport – she plays badminton and squash every week with friends from work, and goes swimming twice weekly. She is an active member of her firm's social club and often goes there with a group of male and female friends in the evenings. If she wants to see a film or play she usually goes to London with her boyfriend as 'there are more things happening there than here' and it also gives her a chance to meet old school friends (she was born in London and her mother still lives there). Saturdays are spent shopping for clothes and going dancing in the evening; on Sundays she goes horse-riding during the morning, spends the afternoon relaxing, and the evening usually at a pub with her boyfriend and other friends. Holidays are usually spent abroad – ski-ing, in the winter, and somewhere with a sunny beach and night life in the summer.

(3) Mrs C

Mrs C lives in a Development Corporation modern terraced home which is obviously freshly decorated (her main hobby is DIY). She moved with her family to Milton Keynes four years previously from a small flat, and much prefers her large house and garden. She is in her late twenties. She has four children, ranging from 3 years to 9 years old; her husband is a garage mechanic. She has no regular paid employment and left school at the minimum age with no exam passes, but occasionally gets part-time work in a shop (usually near Christmas). Although the housework and children keep her busy, she says

> I get bored easily – I'm always decorating and moving the furniture around, and sometimes I make masses of jam, or home made wine.

She would like to get out of the house much more than she does, but has failed her driving test several times, and hates waiting for buses 'all the bus stops round here are next to overgrown paths – very creepy'. She does take the children to the leisure centre, but apart from an occasional swim doesn't participate much herself. 'I hated sport at school – and I don't know many women here to go with – the kids are no help – I'd feel people were staring – even when I swim I think people are laughing at me because I'm not very good'. Also money is a problem – 'most things I'd like to do cost money', and so are the children. 'Sometimes I'd like to go out in the evening – maybe do an evening class or go to the pictures, but he (husband) isn't interested and he won't stay in while I go out'. Her husband is a keen footballer and spends several evenings and a lot of time at weekends training, playing, watching others play and meeting other foot-ballers. This means her weekends are usually full of domestic work, including shopping ('he'll drive the car to the shops but nothing else – and only if he has not got a match to go to') and making sure the children are enjoying their leisure. Her husband is generally fairly unsympathetic to her needs for free time – 'he says I'm at home all day choosing what to do' and they have had no holiday for four years. She has made very few friends in Milton Keynes, although she smiles at neighbours and others she recognizes, and her closest friend lives in London, so she doesn't often see her, although she rings her up most weeks or her friend rings her. Mrs C has plenty of ideas about things she'd like to do – writing children's books, learning about art, for example – but doesn't see how she can do them at present, although 'maybe when the children are older I will'. Apart from taking children to school and the leisure centre her main outings are for shopping and taking the dog for walks 'but I only go in the daytime – it's too frightening at night – he's so soft (dog) he wouldn't help at all if I were attacked'.

(4) Mrs D

Mrs D lives with her husband in an owner-occupied terraced house in one of the established areas of Milton Keynes, and has lived here all her life (the only one of the four for whom this is true). She has never had any paid employment – she is now in her seventies with three grown-up children – but has been involved in community and political groups since the 1920s. Now she is older, she dislikes the thought of segregated activities for OAPs, and hates things like bingo, preferring to be involved with younger people in organiza-tions like the local Peace Campaign. She often has a house full of friends and relatives visiting her. Since her husband retired from his job with British Rail they have both, despite various disabilities (for example her husband has lost most of his sight), continued with or developed hobbies including making children's toys, although as she still has to shop and cook her husband spends more time on this and has never done much in the way of housework. Mrs D does a lot of letter writing, is interested in music and goes to concerts when possible, and has always been fond of sewing. She shares many of her leisure pursuits with her husband, which she thinks is a good thing because she reads only a little (biographies mostly) and doesn't like TV except documentaries and current affairs programmes. Garden-ing in her tiny garden and caring for houseplants is another favourite – she would have like to retire to a bungalow with a larger garden but enough money wasn't available. Holidays used to be spent touring Scotland but since she can't drive (and her husband can no longer because of his deteriorating sight) she mainly sticks to visiting her children or friends. For the last two years she has gone to evening classes in poetry and writing, and has done advanced cookery and floral art as well. Leisure has always been important to her in addition to her household work obligations and she finds she has, if anything, more interests now than when younger.

These four women are all very different in terms of their age, work, lifestyles, interests and backgrounds, but nevertheless certain similarities are apparent – all except Ms B have considerable domestic responsibilities and only in one case are these shared by the men they live with. Mostly they draw on similar kinds of interests and activities – home based crafts and domestic-related activities, cooking, DIY, gardening and different forms of community involvement or traditional 'female' out-of-home interests, with only Ms B involved in sport. For all except Ms B, the lives of others – husbands, children, relatives, friends – are both a constraint and a source of pleasure and enjoyment. Social activities are domestic or revolve around visiting people, others visiting them, or going out mainly in mixed company rather than with other women, to pubs or for meals. Leisure is often fragmented, interspersed with non-pleasurable aspects of the same activity or combined with other activities. Women's participation in the public world is on a very different basis to that of men – there are certain places where women are accepted and feel safe, and in the main women stick to these, although being young and single has some mediating effects. Critical differences between the four women, include age (which clearly does affect the activities done) life cycle (before, during and after child-rearing being crucial here) presence or absence of paid employment (paid employment seems to have an effect on the structuring and scheduling of time and different kinds of work and leisure activity) and differential access to transport (crucially being a driver or non-driver). Level of education is also something which affects leisure activities as well as more obvious factors like employment, although all four women retain an interest in learning through various means. Leisure then is not absent from these women's lives, but it is of a particular kind and takes place within certain structural and ideological boundaries, and in the subsequent chapters some of the wider issues raised by the forms of women's leisure and the boundaries within which it takes place will be explored more fully.

CHAPTER THREE

Leisure in the community

1. Leisure out-of-the-home

In this chapter I am going to look at leisure which takes place *outside* the home, that is leisure in the community, the kind explored in study A in Milton Keynes in the previous chapter. Obviously a new city has some characteristics which are quite different to established residential areas (fewer social networks, less commercial leisure, a more geographically mobile population) and it was suggested that these can and do affect the experiences of leisure of women living there.

However, Milton Keynes, unlike some new towns, in fact combines some characteristics of older towns, because it encompasses older settlements within its boundaries. So, for example, in the research, it became clear that the older towns on the edge of the city were much more important both in providing out-of-home leisure opportunities (including cheaper meeting rooms) and women to organize those activities than were the newer residential areas. In addition, it was apparent that leisure facilities in Milton Keynes were used not only by women who lived there, but also by women from other areas too, including many nearby villages and smaller towns. The contrast between the two samples A and B of women in the Milton Keynes study suggested that some women were much more likely to be involved in out-of-home leisure than others. Many working class women newly arrived in the city, with no paid employment, young children and no private transport were much less likely to be involved in out-of-home leisure than middle class women, those with some form of independent income, those without young children, those living alone and women with access to private transport.

i. Community leisure and the Milton Keynes study

There are two important points which can be drawn from the Milton Keynes study. Firstly, the notion of a community with neat boundaries around it is not very useful in the study of women's leisure, because what constitutes a community varies as much as do women. There is a massive literature on community studies which it is not proposed to discuss here, but the problem of what constitutes a community is hardly a new one. As Graham (1984) notes, for some women, the distance they can walk with a small child may be the boundary of their community. But for women with cars, for instance, what constitutes community may encompass a much bigger mental map and geographical area, perhaps including towns other than the one in which they live. This applied not solely to middle class women either. During my research I encountered a few working class women who were prepared to travel many miles to attend a particular bingo hall or a flower arranging club.

The second point which arises from the Milton Keynes data is that leisure in the community is not something in which all women participate equally. As Green, Hebron and Woodward point out (1985a) there are particular reasons why some women see much community leisure as unavailable to them, quite apart from lifestyle differences, life-cycle stages, and lack of time or money. Lack of transport is one constraint on leisure which affects many women, especially if they have small children, want to travel outside peak times, or at night, or live in (or want to get to) places badly served by public transport. Fewer women than men have driving licences, and not all those who have licences have regular use of a car. But the overriding reason which emerges strongly in both the study of women's leisure in Sheffield conducted from 1983–86 by Green, Hebron and Woodward (and based on an NOP survey of 707 women) and in the Milton Keynes study, is that women do not usually feel free to move around town or city centres alone, especially after dark. In Milton Keynes, because of the combined cycle/footpaths and associated underpasses/heavy shrub undergrowth this is a major problem even in daylight hours. And as Green et al (1985a) say:

> women do not feel comfortable or safe on the streets if they are alone there after dark. They cannot therefore come and go as they please, but have to make careful choices about where they spend their leisure time, and about who they spend it with ... not only was travelling to leisure venues a problem for women ... many women did not feel comfortable inside such venues. The majority of women said they would not feel comfortable going by themselves to pubs, clubs, wine bars or cinemas.
> (Green, Hebron and Woodward, 1985a, p. 37)

Of course, as Brittan and Maynard (1984) point out, moving across a town or city is 'safe' for women when they are accompanied by children or doing domestic tasks like shopping, because these activities are seen as legitimate for women in a way that personal leisure is not. Hence, as Dixey and Talbot observe in their study of bingo (partly based on a community study of Armley in Leeds), it is not necessarily just the intrinsic satisfactions of particular activities such as bingo which attract women, but the context, security and presence of other women at bingo clubs. I found similarly that adult education classes were popular with women in Milton Keynes because they were felt to be safe as well as enjoyable. The Sheffield study discovered that health clubs were places felt to be comfortable and visited by women, especially if those clubs were 'women only' or had sessions specially for women.

ii. Male control over women's out-of-home leisure

It is not however only women who see certain activities and locations as preferable. Men also perceive particular activities and venues as more appropriate than others for unaccompanied women – wives, co-habitees, daughters and women they do not even know. Dances and pubs are seen as much less 'suitable' than bingo or the W.I or a Tupperware party. There are a number of possible explanations which have been advanced to account for the different ways in which men perceive leisure pursuits and locations as suitable for women. Some feminists have argued that the presence of alcohol is a significant factor in determining not only whether women feel 'safe' in a particular leisure location but also whether men are willing to allow women to be there. However, whilst this might seem plausible in relation to places like dance-halls and pubs, cinemas rarely have alcohol available yet are unpopular with women and with men as places for women to go alone, whereas bingo halls and leisure centres which are popular, very often do serve alcohol. A more likely explanation is ironically and systematically linked to the fears women have of being alone in cities or towns. Men's control over women's activities extends to much more than where they allow their wives, girlfriends and daughters to go alone or with other women. As Stanley (1980) has pointed out, men 'police' certain public places where women (except in servicing roles like that of barmaid) are generally unwelcome (this includes many, though not all, pubs and clubs) and it is the presence of men in city or town centres, wine bars and cinemas which makes many women wary of going to those places alone. Indeed the police themselves when cases of rape occur where the offender is unknown, often advise women to 'stay at home' or not travel alone at night, when imposing a curfew on men would be much more effective. Yet it is almost always women and their leisure/freedom which suffers when cases of rape occur. Men's control over women's sexuality and lives effectively limits in many ways what activities are possible for women. Other dimensions of male dominance over women, for example financial control and power over who does what in the house, are major determinates of what leisure time and opportunities are available. And men are usually those responsible for public and commercial provision and planning. So women's leisure in the community is inextricably bound up with men, male control, male leisure and men's ideas about what is appropriate for women. It is also closely linked to age, sexual orientation, ethnicity, income and class.

iii *Mixed and single sex leisure; leisure with children*

If we look at the community leisure activities in which women and men, engage, as opposed to ones which are mostly composed of women only, there is an immediate difference discernible. Community studies and studies of heterosexual couples (Hunt 1980, Leonard 1980, Edgell 1982, Dixey and Talbot 1982) indicate that 'couple leisure' often involves precisely those places and environments which are problematic for women alone (this does not however apply to lesbian couples for whom the latter are still problematic). So pubs, clubs, cinemas, wine bars, restaurants, dances are all a focus of mixed leisure in a way that is rarely considered possible or comfortable for women only (except for young single women). Activities involving children are also ones which may take women to places where, not so accompanied, they would probably feel uncomfortable, although the complex of reasons is rather different. Women will, as we saw in the last chapter, often accompany children to activities or places such as sport and leisure centres where they might not otherwise go. Indeed some women in Dixey and Talbot's study (1982) actually gave as 'their' leisure activities things accomplished only by their children, so vicarious enjoyment is another important feature of women's community leisure. What emerges from a number of studies is that both children and men are seen to have rights to leisure, something that women rarely perceive themselves possessing. Accompanying children to leisure activities is perceived by male partners and men generally as a legitimate part of women's domestic responsibilities. Women going themselves to leisure activities is a different matter.

iv. *Leisure, caring and voluntary organizations*

The question of women's domestic responsibilities brings to light another major facet of women's leisure. As Finch and Groves (1983) show in their collection of readings about women and 'caring', there are strong ideological and structural supports in our society for the idea that caring roles of all kinds are the province of women. Some of these caring roles are in the shape of very demanding forms of unpaid, undervalued work, for example care of the sick, handicapped and elderly infirm dependants. These kinds of caring severely limit the other activities of these responsible in relation to both in-home and community leisure. But whilst some women resent the imposition on them of caring roles by the state and by agencies such as the NHS and social workers (Oliver, 1982), others see caring, as not solely or at all onerous and also undertake voluntary caring activities in the wider community. As Tomlinson (1979) notes, although club membership in general is much greater amongst men than women, certain kinds of corporate groups in the community have been extremely important for women. Such groups include women-only organizations such as Women's Institutes, mothers' groups, and the Women's Royal Voluntary Service, religious groups and hobby clubs. Some of these activities are arranged purely for their leisure potential, whilst others are primarily about caring or fund raising and many more combine leisure with caring work. One form of voluntary organization which more rarely involves women rather than men is the sports club; indeed sport is something from which most women are conspicuously absent on a regular basis and this will be the subject of a separate chapter later.

v. *Life cycles and community leisure*

The final important factor which influences womens' participation in community activities (this isn't to minimize other differences between women related to class, ethnicity and disability) is their stage in the life cycle. Women over forty are the most likely to be involved in voluntary organizations; women who are single and in their teens or twenties are likely to go out a great deal, to be involved in some form of sport and to spend much leisure time in mixed sex groups (if heterosexual). Women in their late twenties and in their thirties with dependent children are, as both the Milton Keynes research and the Dixey and Talbot (1982) study show, least likely to be involved in community leisure on their own account, either with other women or as part of a heterosexual couple. But as Finch (1983a) found in her study of pre-school playgroups, for some working class women playgroups provide a means for snatched leisure, whilst those mothers she terms the 'respectable' mothers, see their task as engaging more seriously with the tasks of making the playgroup work and hence might regard going to playgroup as work or as an extension of their domestic obligations. In the Milton Keynes research there was a certain level of ambivalence about playgroups, which were sometimes enjoyed by women because children enjoyed them or because of the opportunities so afforded for meeting other mothers, but also perceived as a barrier to leisure if they demanded the continuous presence of mothers. The kind of community leisure activities which women engage in are likely to change over the course of their lives. So, the dancing enjoyed by young women becomes something which is no longer possible when they become young mothers because of childcare responsibilities and restrictions placed on them by men (Hobson 1981), but becomes possible again later in life when, as the Sports Council projects about community activities have discovered, tea dances become very popular (*Sport and Leisure* May/June 1985). Then as age starts to impose poor health and restricted mobility on women over seventy, and lack of income is again a serious problem (as it is for young mothers and women outside employment) so community activities start to decrease once more.

2. Community leisure – companions and the use of time

Much of women's leisure takes place in all-women contexts. Of course much male leisure also takes placed in single-sex environments but conventional wisdom has often argued, particularly as an attack on feminism, that women do not like the company of other women, whereas men actively need and seek out the company of other men. However, the available evidence suggests that women also seek out the company of other women and indeed several factors encourage this. These include the gender segregation of the labour market (Garnsey, Rubery and Wilkinson, 1985, Dex 1985) and the isolation of women in carrying out domestic labour (Maynard 1985) as well as traditions involving shared solidarity and experiences between women who are friends or relatives. Additionally, the fears that women have of being alone in urban areas, or public leisure spaces and the ways in which men control the activities of women outside the home, increase the tendency for women to join with other women. Also the difference between the kinds of leisure that women, as compared to men, are interested in, increase the chances that women will spend their out-of-home leisure time with others of their own sex. Of course, women also spend some of their leisure time with children, with men and with people of both sexes, but such shared leisure very often takes different forms from that spent with other women.

Women also have, on average, very much less time at their disposal than men. As *Social Trends* 1985 points out, recent evidence suggests 'female employees had less free time than males, generally because they spent more time on essential activities . . . domestic work, shopping and childcare' (p. 147). For women not in employment the situation is if anything worse, because their so-called free time is often taken up with being 'on call' for various domestic crises which are likely to occur at evenings and weekends (peak leisure time for adult males). Women may also need to cope with the demands made on their household by others' leisure pursuits (washing sports kit, preparing refreshments, chauffering, staying in to enable others to go out). Table 3.1, therefore, only gives us part of the actual situation. The table does however indicate that women have less time for any leisure, whether community based or not. Community leisure of whatever kind, usually requires more time than at-home leisure and may require time to be committed on a regular basis over a quite long period.

It is possible to pick up a piece of knitting for ten minutes, or watch TV whilst ironing, but it is much more difficult to go to a W.I. meeting, or an evening class, or a swim session, in a short time period whose uncommitted nature isn't clear well in advance. Worktime peaks (i.e. those points when work is at its maximum) are also another aspect of women's lives which may make community leisure more difficult. Graham (1984) points out that the periods of maximum work peaks for women are more complex than for men. For employed men with daytime employment, work tends to peak at around 10am and then again at 3pm; their work patterns begin around 7am and finish around 6pm. Women are also busy between those hours, but although there is a fall-off for women not in employment in early afternoon, there is tendency for work to rise again the late afternoon and early evening. A study of shift-working by both sexes reported that women were far more constrained in their leisure by unsocial hours of employment than men (Chambers 1985) but that females were also less likely, because their leisure aspirations were lower, to complain about the effects of working night shifts on their leisure. So to the extent that women's leisure does take place in the community rather than at home, it does so in spite of time constraints and daily lives whose time organization is far more complicated than that experienced by most men.

3 Leisure activities: social and cultural

National evidence on female participation in social and cultural activities presents what seems like quite a rosy picture of women's activities. Indeed Table 3.2 indicates that except for meals and

TABLE 3.1   Time use in a typical week: by economic status, 1982

Hours

	Great Britain					
	Full-time employees		Part-time employees		Housewives	Retired
Weekly hours spent on:	Males	Females	Males	Females		
Employment and travel[1]	45.3	40.7	20.7	22.4	57.7	36.1
Essential activities[2]	23.7	33.5	30.1	48.0	59.2	60.2
Sleep	56.4	57.5	56.6	57.0	51.1	71.7
Free time	42.6	36.3	60.6	40.5		
Free time per weekday	4.0	3.6	7.8	4.7	7.0	9.9
Free time per weekend day	11.4	9.2	10.8	8.6	8.0	11.2

[1]Travel to and from place of work
[2]Essential domestic work and personal care. This includes cooking, shopping, child care, eating meals, washing, and getting up and going to bed.
Source: Leisure Futures Autumn 1983. *The Henley Centre for Forecasting*

Cited in *Social Trends*, p. 147, 1985 Edition. Table 10.1.

TABLE 3.2   Social and cultural activities of males and females, U.K. 1983.

Percentage in each group participating last 4 weeks	males	females
Open air outings		
seaside	7	8
country	3	3
parks	3	4
Entertainment, social and cultural activities		
cinema	7	8
visiting historical builds	8	8
theatre/opera/ballet	4	5
museums/art galleries	3	3
amateur music/drama	3	3
leisure classes	1	2
fairs/amusement arcades	1	2
going out for meal	41	40
going out for drink	64	46
dancing	10	12
Sample size (ie 100% number)	8,751	10,319

SOURCE: General Household Survey 1983; this table taken from *Social Trends* 1985, Table 10.3, p. 149.

drinking, women may do more of these than men. For instance, there are far more women involved in artistic pursuits. (see also Tomlinson 1979) However, not only are the percentages of either sex in most cells extremely small, and give no indication about frequency; the data also do not tell us how many of those activities were carried out because they gave pleasure to the individuals concerned and how many because they involved family outings with children. Going to the seaside, visiting museums and fairs all come into this kind of category. More women than men are also reported as going to the cinema, theatre, opera or ballet, leisure classes and dancing. These findings are broadly consistent with the findings of the Milton Keynes and the Sheffield studies, although such activities are very much a minority taste and are subject to caveats of age/marital status. Shopping and day time walks (often accompanied by children) are popular choices for women in Milton Keynes and

Sheffield (Green, Hebron and Woodward 1985a, 1985b) which do not appear in Table 3.2.

The Dixey and Talbot bingo study (1982) makes clear the extent to which bingo players are drawn from amongst women, and the General Household Survey data for 1983 (see *Social Trends* 1985 p. 152) suggests that the male counterparts of bingo are betting and football pools, although this combination of activities implies that bingo is primarily a gambling pursuit, whilst Dixey and Talbot's (1982) evidence disputes this view of it. The chance to win at bingo is not unimportant, say Dixey and Talbot, but the amounts of money spent by women on bingo are low and the social aspects of the game are as or more important.

Green, Hebron and Woodward in the Sheffield NOP survey also found that across a broad variety of activities, women chose them because they wanted 'the opportunity to chat' and 'have a laugh' (1985a, p. 38), because they wanted 'an escape from the daily routine' and obtained from creative or productive activities a sense of satisfaction and achievement. At the same time the Sheffield researchers point out that, 'making arrangements to spend leisure time outside the home is particularly problematic', (1985a, p. 38) not only because of the time, travel, childcare and domestic constraints already mentioned but also because going out alone or with other women especially to certain locations or activities is a particular source of conflict between women and male partners. The Milton Keynes research suggested that this was less a source of conflict if female relatives rather than friends were involved, or if the going-out included children in the party (which may be one reason mothers join other mothers in the foyers of leisure centres whilst waiting for their offspring to finish various sports).

Of course some of the activities mentioned in the General Household Survey are those which involve heterosexual couples. Forty five per cent of the 'shared' activities between women and male partners in Study A of the Milton Keynes research (although remember this is untypical as it was based on women much involved in out-of-home leisure) revolved round things like going for a drink or meal, whereas hobbies and clubs accounted for much lower percentages of shared leisure (and included women doing books or other clerical/secretarial work for those hobbies and clubs whilst their partner was the active participant). In the second Milton Keynes sample many fewer women reported 'shared' activities with male partners. Young single women also spend much leisure time in the company of men, but as Duquemin (1982) found, this declines quite considerably for older single women who have never been married. Lesbian women are also likely to spend little or no leisure time in the company of men. Wimbush (1985) in a Scottish study found that some couples operated a kind of shift system for their out-of-the-house leisure, where one was out and the other in, at different times of the evening, day or weekend, but this was usually only possible when women were prepared to negotiate this. Some single parents in Wimbush's study had a preference for spending their leisure alone, which was a reaction to having had in the past to fit their leisure round the demands of male partners, or to having had to 'welcome' to their houses people who were friends of their partners rather than themselves.

Most social and cultural out-of-home activities which women engage in therefore, are the choices of a minority of women (I have so far excluded clubs and organizations, many of whose attractions are undoubtedly social, as these are the subject of a later discussion in this chapter). They encompass quite a wide variety, ranging from outings and shopping to creative, aesthetic and artistic or musiscal pursuits. Class doesn't emerge as a strong factor here – either in the Milton Keynes or the Sheffield study. However, those women who do manage these activities often do so in spite of the many constraints which conspire to prevent them getting out of the home at all and often succeed because they have some form of support from others (Wimbush, 1985, Rapaports 1976, 1978). There are many more women who would like to be involved in these activities than actually are, which is apparent from a number of studies including Milton Keynes and Sheffield. There is also a fine line, if indeed one at all, between those out-of-home activities which women undertake because they enjoy them, and those which whilst perhaps enjoyable, are instigated by the needs and interests of others. As one woman in the Milton Keynes study B said about going out for a drink;

> Well I usually go with him (Husband) on a Friday or Saturday . . . it's all right I suppose . . . I can't drink if I've got to drive home . . . it isn't what I'd choose really, I'd rather go with mates from work, but he makes a fuss if I say I don't want to go, and anyway it means I can keep an eye on him, see he doesn't get paralytic.

4. Education as leisure

That women are passionate consumers of adult education is well known and documented not only in research but in official reports on adult and continuing education. Why women are there is another and immensely complicated matter altogether, involving considera-tion of the kind of experiences women have in compulsory schooling (Deem 1980, Spender, 1982, Weiner 1985), their require-ments for education and training (Wickham 1986), what alternative forms of creative and learning activities are available, and the needs of women to do something which raises their own confidence and status. One thing is certain however and that is that they are not there because adult education is an area of learning run for women by women. As Thompson (1983) has pointed out, adult education is just one of the bastions of male privilege and control, despite the fact that 'The women's movement has always had a strong educational component, in the sense that liberation has to be learned as well as created' (1983, p. 16). And if male control is off-putting to middle class women, it is doubly off-putting to working class women, says Thompson. Unlike social activities, educational leisure is significantly shaped by class – most use is made of evening and day classes by middle class women. Those working class women who do return to education remember their schooldays as unpleasant times (Thompson 1983 and McLaren 1982) closely associated with failure, feeling marginal and being told that women's place was in the home.

The explosion of courses designed for or invaded by women over the last few years – NOW (New Opportunities for Women) courses, Second-Chance to Learn, access courses designed to lead onto further or higher education, women's studies courses – have enabled some women to put schoolday memories behind them, although some women still find only conventional, hierarchical, didactic, male domianted classes available to them. There is a great deal of discussion in the conventional literature about adult education and in adult education policy-making circles concerning the vocational/non-vocational division, as though it were possible (almost all local education authorities think it is) to distinguish clearly between pleasurable learning and painful or 'serious' learning. Indeed women are supposed mainly to be interested in the former, possible because some male policy-makers cannot believe women can be serious. But in fact as several feminists have pointed out, the distinction is impossible to sustain when we look at women. Many women do go into adult education with the intention of learning job-related skills, or obtaining qualifications necessary for job hunting, but at the same time, as McLaren's (1982) study of working class women at Hillcroft College found, they also see that education is enjoyable, sociable and an enormous boost to their confidence. In this sense education *is* part of leisure. And as Butler's (1981) study of GCE classes for adults found, examinations are often dreaded and seen as the least valuable part of so called 'vocational' courses. Hence even those classes which are supposedly vocational and lead to certification are taken by some students for whom the certification aspect is perceived as unimportant, but for whom enjoyment of learning about a particular subject is paramount.

The content of evening classes (or day-time classes where these are available) in any case varies enormously, from keep-fit and yoga to cookery and from word-processing to conversational French. But there is usually one difference discernible except for courses which are put on especially for women, like NOW or WOW (Wider Opportunities for Women) courses, much of the pedagogy and organization of so-called vocational courses tend to be geared to passing exams, so that O and A level for example, are often cramming sessions, with students frantically scribbling down notes and having little chance to express their own views. This was something which emerged strongly from the Milton Keynes research. Where students were seen to be actively engaged in their own learning, it was often in classes such as dressmaking, where student expertise matched that of the tutor, or yoga where there is no 'standard' performance to be achieved. Small wonder then that as Thompson (1983) notes, working class women with their unhappy memories of school are not overwhelmingly enthusiastic about joining classes which invoke similar feelings of failure and inadequacy to their school days, and which leave little or no space for them to explore their own interests and experiences.

However, it is a mistake to think that leisure in the form of education is only packaged as something called 'adult education'. When I was doing Study A in the Milton Keynes research something which immediately struck me when I was going to various groups and organizations is that a great deal of learning goes on in those groups and organizations, quite apart from their more obvious intentions and purposes. I have explored this in more detail elsewhere (Deem 1983) but in essence what I found was that the WI, various hobby clubs and even political groups for women were all engaged in some kind of educational process. Often this was itself very traditionally structured, (and the content often conformed to stereotyped female activities – flower arranging, embroidery, sewing, cooking), with a speaker or tutor using fairly didactic methods of putting across their message, and little intervention by the women themselves. But at least women were controlling and organizing that learning as well as benefiting from it. Also such activities were not confined to middle-class middle-aged women, although these were certainly prominent, but also encompassed working class women from their mid-thirties to their late seventies, many of whom would certainly not go to conventional classes. These forms of learning are immensely important in helping women to develop confidence and skills, not only those relevant to a particular topic or subject but also communication skills, although these tend to happen after formal sessions are complete. However it is the case that evening/day classes, and groups which have some kind of educative function are something which only a minority (albeit a large one) of women actually engage in, and in the Sheffield research educational classes hardly figure at all as a major aspect of out-of-home leisure.

Thompson argues that educational classes are not seen as a 'safe' activity for women by male partners, because education may give rise to the challenging of various assumptions, including male dominance of jobs and public life. But in the Milton Keynes study (study A) educational activities were seen as acceptable places to go by both women and where appropriate, their male partners. However this was often only the case as long as attendance at them did not inconvenience the rest of the household. Clearly, developing ideas about women's role, or asking who *should* do the housework, or challenging men's right to go out frequently, or asking questions about the nature of the general social and political world, could be seen not only as inconveniencing the household, but also as fundamentally undermining the structures and beliefs upon which those households were organized. But my research uncovered relatively few women who were exposed to those kinds of ideas, even though my own experience of Open University students suggests that education can be very disturbing to everyday life and beliefs of both student and her household. However, unlike Thompson, I am inclined to think that this effect is not entirely connected to the subject matter being studied; maths classes or a computer course may turn a dependent, passive woman into someone more assertive and confident just as much as a women's studies course. Certainly though, some subjects, especially those with domestic connections, are perceived by men as less threatening, even if learning about them has similar consequences for confidence, because they do not threaten the sexual division of labour in the same way; indeed they may serve to reinforce it.

5. Community and voluntary organizations

Women are amongst the foremost members of community and voluntary organizations. Although as Tomlinson (1979) points out, men are more likely in national surveys to emerge as members of clubs than are women, this not only masks some of the participation by women in voluntary organizations, but also conceals differences in the kinds of organizations men and women are likely to join. Men are, according to the General Household Survey and *Social Trends* more likely to belong to sports clubs, drinking and social clubs than are women (*Social Trends* 1985). They are also more numerous in hobby clubs than women. But the kinds of organizations to which women belong are clustered around women's clubs of all kinds, organizations in the arts field (music, drama, etc.) and organizations connected with voluntary work and caring. *Social Trends* (1985) says:

'Among volunteers in all age groups except those aged 65 or over, women were more likely than men to have done voluntary work regularly' (p. 161). Such is the internalization by women of their 'caring' role in and outside the family that, according to the General Household Survey, female involvement in out-of-home voluntary work is particularly likely to involve the elderly, sick and disabled (*Social Trends*, 1985; GHS, 1981)

There is a class dimension here, although as Dabrowski (1984) notes, voluntary work is not necessarily the preserve of middle class women. Also women *do* belong to some social and hobby clubs. As Dixey and Talbot (1982) demonstrate, bingo clubs have large numbers of female members, and older women (until infirmity, disability or lack of transport stop them) are often avid members of old people's clubs, seeing these as a source of new friends as well as a way to continue existing friendships and interests (Jerrome, 1983). In the Milton Keynes studies (A and B) certain kinds of hobby clubs, especially those connected with domestic and traditional women's crafts were very popular; these included flower arranging clubs which had a particularly working class membership (Deem, 1983). Not all women who mention belonging to a club or voluntary organization are necessarily members out of their own choice; in the Milton Keynes research I found several women who belonged to various sports and hobby clubs who on further investigation turned out to be undertaking secretarial or clerical work for their male partners. This is another example of the kind of process Finch (1983b) refers to in her analysis of how wives are incorporated into their husbands' work, because although a man's interest in a club may be a leisure interest, the tasks performed by his female partner who is doing clerical work for that club are far from a leisure interest, even though some women may rationalize it as such. It may however also be the case that women undertake such tasks in order to spend some time with their partners.

Women's clubs and organizations are, apart from a few exceptions like bingo clubs, the main focus of women's participation in membership of formal groups. As Tomlinson (1979) points out, there are a wide variety of these, from the mostly uniformed and solely caring-oriented Women's Royal Voluntary Society, through the Women's Institutes and Townswomen's Guild which are a mixture of caring, leisure and pressure groups on issues of concern to women, to the National Housewives Register which is leisure-oriented and organizes meetings on almost any topic providing it isn't about housework. It is easy to underestimate the significance of women's organizations to many aspects of women's lives, whether it is leisure or politics or education. Indeed numerically, these groups are the preserve of a minority; they don't figure strongly in the Talbot and

Dixey (1982) study except for elderly women, and they are not prominent in the Sheffield study either. But there are regional and urban–rural differences here too. The Milton Keynes data suggests that for those women who are involved, women's organizations are enormously important, although there are clear age and class patterns to membership. Most members are in the forty-plus age range. Although there are some organizations with a mix of working and middle class women, others are entirely middle class, for instance Ladies Circle and Inner Wheel, which are female counterparts of male organizations mainly devoted to fundraising. But nearly all women's groups are an important source of confidence and enjoyment for their members and as I have already noted, they are in addition a source of learning and education which may or may not be confined to what are traditionally, although incorrectly, seen as 'women's issues and concerns'. Women's organizations are an important aspect of women's participation in the public world even though it is a somewhat differently composed public world to the one which men inhabit. For as Siltanen and Stanworth (1984) point out, the so-called division between the public world which is supposed mainly to consist of men and the private world which is seen to be the province of women, is actually an artificial division. It serves to mask the extent to which women are politically conscious and active by assuming they are confined to the private sphere. Women's clubs and organizations, and also those groups where women form the majority of the membership, are important because they offer the support and companionship of other women. This may be something valued at a particular stage in the life cycle, as for instance in groups concerned with childbirth or those intended for OAPs, or a club available to all women whatever their ages and circumstances. I found that for some women in the Milton Keynes research, the significance of the groups they belonged to lay not in the objectives and content of the meetings themselves, but in a chance to sit somewhere in the warm, away from domestic duties and worries, just talking to their friends and without having to take the supportive or invisible roles women often play in mixed sex conversation (Spender 1981, French and French 1984). This was the case as much for WI members who wait impatiently for the formal parts of their meetings to end, as for old ladies attending flower arranging clubs who arranged themselves at the back of the room where they could neither hear, nor see very well the various demonstrations put on, but where they could talk undisturbed. Women's groups are a 'safe' place to go, away from men and are often seen by men as acceptable places for women to be in when they are not at home, although this is to minimize the extent to which women find it possible to escape from their domestic duties to attend meetings on a regular basis. Like other leisure activities getting time to go is often the subject of much conflict and negotiation in houeholds and with male partners.

6. Sports clubs and sport

I am not going to dwell on this topic at this point because it is the subject of the next chapter in the book. But it will suffice to say here that for most women taking part in sport is not something of significance in their lives. I found few women who belonged to sports clubs in which they were active participants, but rather more were members of leisure centres (but still a tiny minority of the two samples). The Sheffield and Leeds studies (Green, Hebron and Woodward 1985a, 1985b, Dixey and Talbot 1982) confirm the low levels of membership of sports clubs and low rates of participation, although the Sheffield study did find that health clubs were seen as relatively safe leisure venues for unaccompanied women.

7. Holidays

Unlike some of the activities explored so far, holidays are usually assumed to be unambiguously leisure activity. However this is far too simple a view of what most holidays involve. As Tysoe (1985) notes, 'People go on holiday not just to meet new people . . . but also . . . to improve relationships within their own family. Sadly, this may not work' (Tysoe, 1985, p. 230). Not only may holidays reproduce, sometimes in a more antagonistic form, all the tensions and conflicts of domestic life, but also, and as importantly for women, they may *not* mark an end to domestic and childcare obligations. Also we can only *assume* that women are as equally likely to go on holiday as men, and here the national surveys and *Social Trends* are unhelpful because there is no gender breakdown. So, in 1983 the British National Travel Survey by the British Tourist Authority found 42 per cent of adults had taken no holiday that year, and that the proportion was much higher amongst working class people (presumably defined by male jobs) rising to 58 per cent of class D and E, whereas only 22 per cent had taken no holiday in classes A and B (*Social Trends* 1985). Many women do go on holiday with their families, but this doesn't necessarily hold for single women whether they have dependent children/relatives or not. However what is clear is that unlike full-time employed workers whose annual holiday entitlement is going up (95 per cent of manual employees by 1983 received at least four weeks per year *Social Trends* 1985) housewives have no holiday entitlement, and many women in part-time work will find themselves with no or reduced holidays because holidays for part-time workers are often calculated in different and less advantageous ways. Additionally, employed women with dependent children or relatives may find themselves having to use up holiday leave to cope with unexpected domestic crises. So just in terms of the possibilities of taking holidays, women are already disadvantaged.

If we begin to examine in detail the context, content and experiences of holidays for women, they do not always decide where or when. Edgell (1982) found in his study of middle class couples that decisions about where to go were usually joint decisions, but this may not be the case in working class families. Nor are joint decisions (as Edgell partially recognizes) always made on a basis of equality between the decision makers even if *they* say this is the case. Hunt's study of a mining village in Staffordshire (1980) found that women in employment often put money away from their wages to help pay for holidays, but this in itself does not guarantee them a major part in deciding where to go. The Sheffield NOP study (Green, Hebron and Woodward, 1985b), Dixey and Talbot (1982) and my own Milton Keynes sample B all found that about 70 per cent of women had been on some kind of holiday of at least four days to a week's duration, during the relevant years. Some had been away more than once, mostly those from middle class households, including 22 per cent in the Sheffield study and about 15 per cent in the Milton Keynes random sample (nationally 20 per cent in 1983).

In the Dixey and Talbot (1982) study the commonest destination for women with families on their main holiday, was to seaside resorts in the North of England, with holiday camps, camping and caravanning as popular choices, rather than hotels or boarding houses which were felt to be too expensive. So holidays frequently meant some kind of self-catering, which as the researchers point out, means women still have to work when they are away. Both male partners (usually in terms of fixed holiday dates) and children were felt to constrain choice of where and when a holiday occurred. Dixey and Talbot noted preference often being given, where there were young children, to a holiday that was more suited to children's tastes than adults. Holiday camps may combine both adult and child tastes which is one reason for their choice; Harris (1985) found that ethnic minority households and those with handicapped children chose a holiday camp too, because in the large size and anonymity they were less likely to encounter prejudice (or perhaps were less aware of it) and unpleasantness. Despite the growing numbers of British residents holidaying abroad (in 1971 only 36 per cent of the adult population had ever been on holiday abroad, but it had risen to 62 per cent in 1983) Harris found 'going abroad' was felt to be more suited to young single people or those without dependent children.

In the Sheffield study Green *et al* (1985b) found 51 per cent who either camped or stayed in self-catering flats/houses, and 37 per cent who stayed in a hotel, but the percentages camping or caravanning were greater amongst working class women and those with young children. In the Milton Keynes study I found one third of sample A had gone on camping or caravanning holidays, and nearly half who had stayed in a hotel, but in sample B which contained more working class women, this was exactly reversed. I also asked group B women what they would prefer to do as opposed to what they actually did, and most of those who camped (but not many of those who caravanned in their own caravan) would have preferred a hotel. Once on holiday actual and ideal preferences came closer together, with walking, dancing, sitting on a beach and sightseeing most preferred, but often much less time was *actually* spent on these activities than was felt desirable. Many women were all too aware that they spent as much or more time doing domestic work on holiday as they did the rest of the year, and usually with fewer and less reliable labour-saving gadgets to help. Men's contribution to holiday labour was often said to be limited to fetching bread and milk from the shops and 'cooking' on a barbecue, but on touring caravanning holidays men almost always did the driving. Towing caravans is *not* women's work. The sexual division of labour thus lives on in holiday contexts. Holidays are not necessarily leisure for women unless they go alone or with other women, but may be an extension of their normal domestic and childcare responsibilities; nor are they necessarily a rest from tensions and conflicts within households or families.

8. Women and community leisure; conclusions

This chapter has tried to focus both on the constraints which face women who participate in community or out-of-home rather than home-based leisure and the typical forms which female out-of-home leisure takes. Although it has been made clear that women do differ, and that class, income level, children, life cycle stage, employment, household composition, sexual orientation, age and ethnicity can have a strong influence on what is possible and what is seen as enjoyable, it is also apparent, as Brittan and Maynard (1984) citing Poggi and Coormaert's work, say:

> the fact that all women have restricted use of the city creates a common denominator between them. Women of all social categories are affected. (Brittan and Maynard, 1984, p. 126–7)

So that although different women, and even the same women at different stages in their lives, are likely to 'choose' different activities, those choices are made within the limits of male patriarchal control over women and mostly on the basis of gender-typed socialization, as well as within the context of what publicly financed and commercially provided facilities and activities are available in capitalist societies (i.e. there aren't usually women–only bars or cinemas, or females–only night transport). There is thus an ideological and a material basis to women's community leisure, and there is also a merging of the so-called public and private dimensions of women's lives in that leisure. Brittain and Maynard suggest that the distinction between these two dimensions, public and private, is worthy of some re-examination, because while the distinction is sometimes important at a descriptive level, (just as I find it useful to distinguish between community-based and home-based leisure) its use in analysis and theorizing needs much more careful thought because the two dimensions are so intertwined. In this instance, there is a close analytical relationship between women's lives at home and their lives outside the home, and between the power and control mechanisms which are at work in the household and those operating in the wider community. But also the connections are more than analytic, because although a woman who goes out for the afternoon or evening leaves her kitchen sink and/or children/older dependents behind, the responsibilities and obligations which they represent are still present in her head and ideologies about women's role continue to have an effect on what she does, how she does it, with whom and the extent of her enjoyment.

At the same time however we need to remain conscious of the fact that, whatever the reasons and determinations of women's community leisure and no matter how well or badly (and as I shall develop in a later chapter, it often is badly) she is provided for by what is available, there are many positive aspects to women's leisure in the community. These included pleasure, the companionship of other women, the possibility of learning new knowledge and skills, the development of confidence to be outside the home, and relaxation. So in looking at the negative aspects of female community leisure, including the reinforcement of gender stereo-typed roles and attitudes, it is important to recognize that women do derive real enjoyment and benefit from their leisure outside the home. The point is not to take away or denigrate the activities involved, but to develop a better understanding not only of the constraints facing women but also of how more women might be enabled to take part in out-of-home leisure and how what is available to women can be improved and increased. This is something to which I shall return in the next chapter, where the focus will be on sport.

CHAPTER FOUR

Women and sport

I have deliberately chosen to devote a separate chapter to women and sport, because I think it is a form of leisure which is both distinguishable from other forms of leisure and is shaped by rather different factors and considerations. Sport, even in contemporary industrial societies, is still largely dominated by men at every level, from those for whom sport is a way of earning a living rather than a leisure activity, through those for whom it is a hobby, to those who are spectators rather than participants. Also sport, like many other aspects of our society, is largely organized and administered by men. For a long time there were thought to be sports which women could not participate in or in which women could not hope to excel; biology and physiology received the blame for this, although as both research and the actual performances of women in sport have demonstrated over the last ten years, women are better suited physiologically to certain sports (including marathon running) than men and are also fast catching up with male performances in sectors like athletics (Ferris 1981, Dyer 1982 and Lustig 1985). Indeed as Talbot (1984) notes, women's

> sex, their biological definition of being female, does not prevent them from being competent sports players. And yet, in the 1980s the Sports Council in Britain has targeted women in its ten year strategy, on the grounds that the potential for growth is highest among women because their present participation rate is low. I would argue that *gender* – the socially constructed, normative conception of male/female status – is therefore a central focus for consideration of the relationship between women and sport. (Talbot 1984, p. 2)

In other words it is *not* biology which is responsible for women's low sport participation, but rather the social and economic conditions imposed on women which determine their lack of interest in sport.

Sport thus appears no different to any other form of leisure. But sport *is* different from other kinds of leisure in at least four ways.

65

Firstly, it has a national and international significance which most other forms of leisure do not have, because of the media coverage and the amount of sport played. Secondly, sport, unlike most forms of leisure, is actually specifically taught in schools, and is in fact one of the most gender-segregated areas of the curriculum (Leaman 1984, Scraton 1986). Thirdly, there is an ongoing debate about the importance of connections between sport and physical fitness and health. Fourthly, sport is often associated with competitiveness and aggression as well as with masculinity. Sport is in fact not marginal to the lives of some women, but the kinds of sport women participate in are on the whole different from those in which men participate, women are often excluded from male-dominated sports even if they want to participate, and many women switch off from sport in their early teens whilst still at school (Scraton 1985, 1986). Those few who do continue are likely to reduce or cease involvement in sport when they have children or get married. Yet potentially sport, of all kinds, is an important form of leisure activity for women, which offers many benefits including enjoyment, skills, development of physical strength, flexibility and co-ordination, a positive body image, and a contribution to well-being and fitness. Although still very controversial, there is also some small-scale research which indicates that exercise may be a useful antidote to women suffering from depression (Mutrie 1985).

Yet as early results from research by Wimbush (1985) on a sample of young Scottish mothers show, lack of fitness and tiredness may be one reason why physical sports and activities which are not work-related are avoided by women. Other barriers to participation include many of those factors central to explaining why women have in general less leisure than men – domestic responsibilities, lack of money, transport and facilities and a concerted attempt by men to exclude women from places where male sport occurs. Like leisure, sport is very much bound up with men, with patriarchal power relations and male-related definitions of the relationship between paid work and free time usage; sport is also very closely linked to notions of masculinity, virility and physical strength. Against this rather pessimistic picture however, needs to be set both the participation of women in newer and non-competitive forms of sport – yoga, jogging, aerobics – and the many initiatives and projects currently being set up by the Sports Council and other groups/ organizations which are intended to increase both the opportunities available to women and their participation.

1. In which sports do women participate?

The national surveys suggest that the most popular sports amongst adult women are walking, swimming, keep-fit and darts (*Social Trends* 1985, quoting the 1983 General Household Survey). Whereas amongst men, walking also emerges as the most popular, other activities which are popular include billiards and snooker, swimming, darts, football, golf and squash, although for both sexes the percentages of people of all ages participating in sport does not exceed 17 per cent of the population for women and 19 per cent for men. Nevertheless this very general evidence suggests that women tend to opt for non competitive sports and those which can easily accommodate other family members, whilst men prefer competitive sports (walking and swimming excluded) and those which typically occur in all male environments. It is also fair to say that participant sport is not a majority interest for either sex in the U.K. For males and females the participation rates are highest amongst the 16–19 age group, but the decline in participation after that age is much less marked for men than for women.

When we come to look at the evidence from studies specifically concerned with women we find a not too dissimilar picture. In the Milton Keynes sample A, the most favoured sports were walking, swimming, yoga and keep-fit, badminton and squash. But this sample was intentionally biased towards those women for whom a significant part of their leisure takes place out of the home, which explains the appearance of two sports which require both equipment and facilities as well as some knowledge of the skills involved. In response to questions about leisure activities which have been given up, Sample A women instanced sport in general, along with dancing and swimming at the top of the list and not only amongst the older age-groups. A typical response is summed up by the following comment;

> I used to be a keen swimmer and also played hockey for a local team when I was in my early twenties. That all stopped when I started courting – my boyfriend wanted me to spend my time with him. I did think I'd start swimming again – in fact I did go when I was pregnant – but then afterwards it wasn't the same – I did take the eldest to Mums and tods swimming but it was her that did the swimming not me – when you've been really good at something you can't be satisfied by doing it half-heartedly – a couple of lengths was all I could manage, so I decided it wasn't worth it. The main exercise I get now is running after the kids and the occasional walk on a Sunday – and to tell you the truth I get so tired I couldn't face anything more strenuous – I can't imagine how I used to play hockey at all!' (woman in early thirties, two children under seven, husband an engineer).

Even where sport has been liked and enjoyed, lack of support from the rest of the household and the responsibilities imposed by children often sound the death knell. The woman just quoted nevertheless had a husband who still played football regularly and whose only period without active sports involvement had been six weeks three years ago when he broke his leg!

If sport was never attractive in the first place, few reasons are needed to stop all physical activity except that strictly necessitated by the daily routine, although often the point at which children enter their teens may be one at which a keep-fit class or something similar is taken up. In the Milton Keynes sample B less than one-third of the 168 women involved took part in any sport other than walking and most of that walking fell well below the 'At least two miles' criterion used by the General Household Survey. Amongst the thirty percent who did do some form of sport, swimming, yoga and keep-fit were the most likely choices. Swimming is often chosen because it does fit in with children's own leisure interests, and as the woman I just quoted points out, when children are small the amount of swimming that an accompanying adult can do is minimal. For many women in the two Milton Keynes studies I carried out, sport was either something done by their male partners on Sundays or weekday evenings, or it was something you infrequently watched on TV (usually when there was no alternative viewing). A group of women from a local organization had this to say about sport; 'It's what men do isn't it . . . it was bad enough at school having to play all those ghastly games and run around in a silly games skirt freezing to death but when there's a choice . . .'.

However it is important not be misled by this notion of 'choice'. Yes, many women do 'choose' not to do sport. They also, as we have already seen, may 'choose' not to have much leisure. In both instances the choice is a forced one and is closely related to structures of male power over women as well as to prevailing ideologies about masculinity and feminity. One reason why women do not choose sport is because it is closely associated with masculinity, male aggression, status and power; it is not seen as something for women. Even those women for whom sport has an appeal may not actually keep up their participation rate as they move into their thirties and forties. Here the significant factor is likely to be their heavy burden of domestic labour and childcare (despite in most cases having an adult male around) plus lack of independent money and transport. When women do participate it is often in a sport which reinforces traditional ideas about femininity – yoga, keep fit, swimming – and which are hence compatible with stereotypes of beauty, grace and female attractiveness. What is much less rarely acceptable is women doing sports which involve physical contact, getting dirty or sweating profusely, or having to wear unfashionable clothes. A P.E. teacher interviewed by Scraton (1986), asked her views about girls playing soccer said 'I have yet to see an elegant woman footballer. Maybe I'm just prejudiced but they just look horrible.' Another P.E. teacher said 'I don't think soccer is a girls' sport – physical contact and all that rolling in the mud' (Scraton 1986, p. 20). As Hargreaves (1985) notes, 'In sport, 'masculine' identity incorporates images of strength, aggression, muscularity and activity, but it implies, at the same time, an opposite, 'feminine' identity, associated with relative weakness, gentleness and grace . . . It seems to follow logically that men are 'naturally' better suited to sport' (Hargreaves 1985, pp. 26–27).

In the Sheffield study only 23 per cent of the 707 sample of women surveyed played some kind of sport, and once again swimming was very popular (Green, Hebron and Woodward 1985b). Other choices for women who did enjoy sport included badminton, tennis, running and squash. But participation was least amongst older women, working class women and those with low incomes—very similar to the Milton Keynes findings that it is mostly middle class women in their twenties to forties with some money of their own, or childless single young women, for whom sport is most attractive.

2. Sport and the life cycle

Life cycle stage is particularly influential on sport and the Sheffield researchers found (1985a,b) that women under twenty five were most likely to play sport and go to keep-fit; ironically they are probably the fittest group anyway. But sport is often also a social activity – it tends to be done by friends together or families – and hence yoga and keep fit, which are usually done in classes, may owe some of their popularity to the fact that like bingo you can go alone, but be part of a group once you get there. Also significant from the findings of the Sheffield study was the revelation that of those public leisure venues where women would feel comfortable going alone, only sports and health clubs emerged as locations where a substantial minority of the sample would feel happy going alone; 46 per cent of the total sample would feel comfortable (Green, Hebron and Woodward 1985a, 1985b). This clearly has implications for policies on leisure and for commercial as well as public provision and indicates that there may be a great potential for increasing female sport participation through providing women-only 'safe' accessible facilities.

3. Women's sporting roles

Dixey and Talbot (1982) in their study of Armley (unlike the Sheffield researchers who found that where women claimed to participate in sport, they did so on a regular basis) found that only a tiny proportion of the women claiming that they were involved in sport were so doing on a regular basis. Whilst 37 per cent of their sample said that they took part in sport, less than 5 per cent had sport as part of their regular weekly routine. Swimming was by far the most frequently mentioned sport, followed by walking, badminton, squash and riding. Dixey and Talbot suggest that in fact women are much more likely to be involved in sport as an ex-participant, often far distant and forgotten about 'I've never been a participator in sport. Well . . . those days are long past – I used to play in Leeds city netball team when I was a gangling schoolgirl' (Dixey and Talbot, 1982, p. 59). The other significant role played by women in sport in the Leeds study, and a finding which very much tallies with the Milton Keynes research, is as a parent and servicer of children who play sport and as a servicer of husbands who rarely find that marriage and childrearing, let alone housework, interfere with their sport. This can be a particular problem where a male partner is heavily committed to a sport as was this woman's husband;

> He goes training on a Thursday night and plays on a Saturday afternoon and a Sunday morning. We have endless arguments about that. He does work late quite often so he doesn't get to see Joanne (child) during the week and I think weekends, at least one full day . . . should be with the family (Dixey and Talbot, 1982, p. 60).

The researchers found that other women did go to sports events as spectators, but as the writers perceptively point out, there are two types of participant – the active one who *chooses* to go along to watch, and the by-stander, who may watch reluctantly either because they are prevented from playing (for example snooker and billiards in a working men's club) or because they are carrying out a servicing role (cricket club teas, chauffeur, confidence booster, half-time refreshments etc.). Wimbush (1985) in her study of Scottish mothers found that there were a number of factors influencing women's views about sport, physical activity and fitness. Women with self confidence felt good about their bodies but were in a minority, whereas a large number of women were found to be pre-occupied with their weight and lacked self-confidence because of this, especially after childbirth. For some this feeling of being overweight was an encouragement to take up some kind of sport, but for most others it deterred them completely. Fitness was mostly defined as being able to get through their daily routine – a long way removed from the kind of definition a sports player might give. All the evidence then points to the fact that only a minority of women are involved in sport, that the kinds of sports done are almost never team games, rarely involve competition, are apart from walking usually done alone or in the company of children or other women and are frequently activities which are seen by women and by men as 'appropriate' because they incorporate and even help develop notions of grace, passivity, elegance and beauty rather than sheer physical strength, aggression, or power. I want now to turn in a little more detail to the barriers to women's participation in sport, where we can learn not only from women who play little sport but also from those few who are keen sportswomen.

4. Barriers to female participation in sport

There are actually two ways of looking at this. One is to examine why women don't participate. The other is to compare and contrast those women who do participate with those who don't. Wimbush (1985) while not specifically concerned with sport, has outlined some characteristics which seem to her to be connected to women's ability to control their time. These include work routines, support from others, an ability to ignore the expectations of others, self-confidence, having social contacts, possessing money and where applicable being independent of their partner. I would suggest that some of these are especially important to sport participation. Those women in my Milton Keynes sample A who *were* highly involved in sport did have the support of others in their households or families, were able to bracket away conventional notions of femininity and ignore the insults and beliefs of others, were confident both of themselves and of their bodies. They were not always single middle-class women either; this was particularly true of those involved in athletics and sports like judo which seem more likely to attract working class participants. Women who had become committed to a particular sport seemed to stand out in much the same way as do other individuals who have done something most people would find difficult.

There was nearly always someone, a friend, parent, coach who had been particular influential in bringing about the choice of a particular sport in the first place and then fostered its development. A similar pattern may be found in female school pupils who make non-traditional choices of subject in the later years of secondary schooling (Deem 1986). However in sport it is not only those women who make non-traditional choices who need sponsoring and supporting. Clarke and Critcher (1985) assert that certain kinds of sport are not seen as threatening in gender terms; 'Those physical activities which stop short of real sport and remain as recreations are perceived as less of a gender threat. Jogging, cycling and hiking are less likely to be challenged as legitimate female leisure' (Clarke and Critcher 1985, p. 162). But in fact a woman who is *serious* about at least two of the three sports they mention is likely to be perceived of as threatening male power and superiority over women; witness the efforts to keep women out of the Olympic marathon event and the attempts by the male cycle racing fraternity to suggest that women are unsuitable as racing cyclists. Women are only acceptable as serious participants in sports which are almost entirely female-dominated (yoga, gymnastics, synchronized swimming) and as dabblers in other sports; it is all right for a woman to cycle round the park but not for her to want to take part in the Paris–Roubaix or the Tour of Lombardy races. There is not nearly enough research material available yet on women in sports for us to generalize, but my own very limited evidence does suggest that women who continue sports involvement are often either single or based in households where there is wide support (and often wide participation too) for the activity in question. Other people, both men and women, are likely to see keen women sports participants as odd or as deviant, although this is of little concern to the women themselves, which is precisely why they are able to sustain a level of commitment more usually found in men. A woman in my sample who was a judo instructor told me; 'Yes, they are all involved, even the youngest . . . my husband is also an instructor, in fact that's how I met him and he has always encouraged me (do your friends think it's odd that you spend all your time on judo?) – yes some of them do, but I tell them they ought to go out and do something instead of vegetating in front of the tele every evening.'

Women who do not participate in sport can for the sake of convenience be categorized into two groups – those who do no sport because they dislike it and those who do no or very little sport because they are prevented by various constraints, but who would like to do a sport, or play an existing sport on a more regular basis. However there is no hard and fast boundary between these two groups in the sense that similar factors can be seen to have led to their attitudes towards sport. Scraton (1985, 1986) and Fletcher (1984) have begun the process of documenting both how physical education for teachers and girls has developed historically and how it operates now, showing the stereotyped notions of femininity which are still incorporated within it, both at the teacher training level and within schools. As Scraton points out (1986) although PE has given women a freer development of physical exercise and thus increased the chances of access to sport and recreation, it has done so largely within 'dominant ideologies relating to physical ability and capacity, motherhood and sexuality' (Scraton 1986 p. 5) so that the 'freedom' offered has been a fairly confining one. In the four schools in one LEA studied in depth by Scraton, she found a heavy emphasis in the ethos and content of PE teaching, on preparing girls to be wives and mothers, and teaching them to dress and behave as young ladies; 'Walk in properly. Imagine you are in a beauty parade.' was a not untypical remark made to girls returning to the changing rooms from their lessons. Great emphasis was also placed on appearance; 'I teach them to have correct uniform, kit, hair tied back, attention to detail'. . . Women's bodies are thus supposed to be physically developed to look good to men, but protected from 'over-development' which is 'unattractive' (to men). Thus physical contact sports are eschewed and anything developing muscle is seen as unnatural. However as recent research (Dyer 1982) shows, women's bodies may actually be much less vulnerable to injury through sport than men's.

Not only is school PE for girls bound up with ideas about motherhood and feminine sexuality; it is also the case that many girls resent the emphasis on exposing their bodies, the discipline imposed, the clothes demanded and the ordeal of showers which are part and parcel of school PE (Scraton 1985). Peer group culture operates to ensure that most girls reject sport and physical activity early in their teens, many never to return. Sport is associated with unpleasant games lessons, being embarrassed in the showers, dressing in silly clothes and above all it is associated with being masculine or at any rate unfeminine. Not only this, but as Talbot (1984) has pointed out,

> 'whilst some *boys* games become or service *men's* sports, most *girls* games do not relate to *women's* sports, partly because of their inherent characteristics; partly because of women's lack of power to institutionalize; partly because women's sports tend to be adapted from men's; and most significantly of all because of the discontinuity between being a girl and being a woman' (Talbot, 1984, p. 5).

Hence there are relatively few girls who leave school either with an interest in sport which they will want to continue with (and if the latter occur the chances are that the skills will not anyway have been learnt at school).

Once women have left full-time education their involvement in sport begins a downhill descent from which it never recovers. Young women are often preoccupied with fashion, music and boyfriends. Whilst for a few, sport may continue in this phase, as Leonard's (1980) research on engaged couples in Wales demonstrates, once serious relationships are established many of the woman's interests tend to decline, although her male partner is much more likely to continue his, including sport. Thereafter, with marriage, and children, the sporting roles taken up are most likely to be those referred to earlier-spectator and servicer of others involved in sport. Many of the same factors which restrict women's leisure are responsible for women not taking a more active role in sport. Although facilities may be available in the shape of sports centres and so on, they are often expensive, have no childcare provision (or only in the daytime, not at weekends or evenings) are difficult to get to by public transport and are often perceived as unwelcoming to the novice or inexperienced. Sport requires time, something that as we have already seen, many women do not have much of; when they reach an age when their home commitments and work obligations *are* lessening, declining physical powers and or ill-health are likely to mean that sport is not something which is turned to. Because sport is seen largely as a male preserve, and is controlled by men, women lack the kind of servicing and support which many male sports players receive from their female partners. This is particularly true of working class women whose housework, childcare and paid jobs are likely to leave them exhausted and wanting to spend any free time they have in a passive rather than an active way (Westwood, 1984). In my Milton Keynes interviews a woman in her early thirties with two children, one ten, the other twelve, said of her attempts to go jogging:

> Well first of all I tried going early in the mornings but then everyone complained I was making them late by enjoying myself rather than getting on with breakfast. Then I thought I'd go at lunchtime – but the girls at work laughed at me and anyway I have to shop most days – so finally I decided I'd try the evenings – after we'd eaten I'd wait an hour or so and then go – that was OK in the summer but of course now its dark I don't feel safe – also Ron (husband) doesn't much like me running anyway – he says I'm getting leg muscles and that feminine women don't get all sweaty.

Even though this woman was unusually determined it still wasn't really possible. For many others sport wasn't even considered;

> Sport? I'd never have the energy – it takes me all I've got to do the house, look after the kids and go to work – the only thing I like to do in the evenings is sleep or watch a video (woman in late twenties, three children, job as an office worker, Milton Keynes interviews).

As Wimbush (1985) has correctly perceived, women's own sense of wellbeing, health and fitness is vital to whether or not they engage in leisure and sport. Body image is another powerful barrier to sport participation. Women are often over-concerned with their weight (Kerr and Charles 1986, Orbach 1982, Wimbush 1985) and may not want to expose their bodies because they are felt to be ugly and not sexually attractive (there is also a very real fear even from women who have a more positive body image, that they will experience sexual harassment as a result of their sport–runners and joggers are especially likely to suffer from this). As Graydon (1983) and Talbot (1984) have both noted, women who participate in sport are supposed to be 'feminine' and if they are not then they are exposed to insults and derision.

> Overtly hostile attitudes are expressed in several ways. . . . One way of doing this is to cast doubt on the sex of a top-ranking participant. In the 1960s the Press sisters of the Soviet Union were the victims of this brand of publicity. Rumour abounded that the Press sisters were really men and in the ensuing turmoil the Olympic sex test was instigated. This test . . . is performed only on competitors entering for events restricted to women, its implication being that if you're that good, then maybe you're a man (Graydon, 1983, p. 9).

Media coverage of women's sports often feels it necessary to comment, irrelevantly, on physical attributes or their off-sports field predilictions for make-up and pretty clothes, or else stresses their domestic role; 'Mary Decker . . . has become sporting America's favourite daughter; not just as little Mary Decker, hammer of the sickles, but also as pretty, sexy, Mary Decker who, in this Amazonian world, wears make-up on the track and shaves her legs' (Freedman, 1984, quoted by Talbot 1984); 'Joyce Smith, (marathon runner) mother and housewife, was last week winding down her training' (Doust 1982, quoted by Graydon 1983). Women who do not conform to acceptable 'feminine images are discouraged from doing sport or are seen as having a 'male' approach.

There has been a tendency on behalf of bodies like the Sports Council and other organizations trying to increase women's participation in sport, to see the main barriers as being facilities and opportunities. Women's lack of interest in sport is as much due to the stranglehold which men have over sport (its image, its management and participation) as to poor facilities, as the Women's Sports Foundation (founded in 1984) has been at pains to point out. But patriarchal power relations with regard to sport do not stop with sport itself; they extend to the ways in which men perceive women either as housewives and mothers or sex-objects, and to the manner in which men develop strategies to control women's behaviour and sexuality. Thus the only way in which significantly more women are likely to come to see sport as something which is both enjoyable and in which they have a right to participate is to actually change the nature of the social relationships and male power which surround sport itself. Sports goods and clothing for women also reinforce gender stereotypes – pink shoes, 'pretty' bicycles. An examination of some of the efforts being made to increase female sport involvement follows, but this point concerning the need for more wide reaching changes to society as well as to sport should be borne in mind when analysing these efforts.

5. Bringing women in to sport

There are three main types of strategy; one aims to introduce more women to existing 'female' sports, whether these are activities like yoga and keep-fit, or activities like dancing which not everyone would recognize as sport, but which do involve considerable physical exertion. The second tries to introduce women to sports which have traditionally been done largely by men. The third tries to actually do something about the male domination over sport and is thus in that sense trying to achieve rather more than just increase female participation rates, which is important but which will not in itself achieve the more fundamental changes which are necessary if women are to claim space in sport. There is also as well as these three types of intervention, an effort to look at the specific problems faced by women active in sport with regard to injuries (Grigson 1985) and pregnancy. The Sports Council covers the first two categories of intervention strategy and has concentrated on women as a target group in a number of its initiatives, including the ten year strategy, the 'Ever thought of sport' for the under 25s and the 'Over Fifties' campaign. Women have also been included in various regional initiatives in the sport and community developments, some of which have concentrated on areas of high unemployment, thus displaying all the features of what Clarke and Critcher (1985) call sport as 'compensation'. That is, schemes are aimed at the unemployed and other potentially idle or disruptive groups as a compensation for having no job, for having low incomes or living in socially deprived areas (Glyptis 1985). In fact as might be expected, since women are much less likely to be perceived as part of such 'dangerous' groups as the unemployed in our society, 'compensation' schemes have attracted relatively few women. Having time on their hands is generally only a problem for older women who have been made redundant (Martin and Wallace 1984) and such women are unlikely because of their age to join in sport anyway, if it has never been part of their adult lives. Younger women without jobs may not perceive themselves as being unemployed if they are mothers and in any case tend to have many other forms of unpaid work with which to occupy their time.

Fitzjohn and Tungatt (1985) surveying various projects to encourage women into sport, note that projects involving women only have been successful in places like Norwich and Cambridgeshire and that women have usually been in the majority in some other successful mixed projects too. The importance of making provision for childcare and of basing projects in places where women go, for example health centres, are emphasized. Things like tea dances, even where held in the unlikely venue of a Working Men's club have also proved attractive to older and some younger women. But some of the projects merely serve, whilst encouraging more women, to reinforce female stereotypes–elegant women taking part in aerobics together with those who feel they ought to be more elegant–and don't move away from the traditionally feminine activities which some women already do (yoga, keep-fit, aerobics). Most sports which women are encouraged into in later life are non-competitive (or can be played in that way, for example tennis and badminton) although there is an argument here about whether in fact competitive sport is always necessarily to be seen as masculine and therefore undesirable. Efforts to get women interested in sports dominated by males are often successful at the initial stage of teaching skills, but founder when the course or project ends, because clubs and groups of men involved with the sports concerned do not want women encroaching on their territory. Thus it is important to recognize that putting on low cost, easy access, childcare provided, conveniently-timed courses in places where women feel comfortable going is only *part* of the process of *beginning* change, or else the effects are only likely to be very temporary.

The Women's Sports Foundation set up in 1984, aims to 'promote the interests of all women in and through sport and to gain equal opportunities and options for women' and it is concerned to point out that in order to do this power needs to be wrested away from vested male interests in sport. It is also attempting to alter the huge amount of discrimination which women in sport experience, from media prejudice to being effectively shut out from sports clubs and organizations. Such discrimination may be explicit (e.g. snooker and pool rooms in working men's clubs, where women are actually barred, as private clubs are exempt from the 1975 Sex Discrimination Act), or implicit, in that women trying to take part in male sports are sexually harassed, as Graydon points out happened to the marathon runner Kathy Switzer when she was the first woman to run the 1967 Boston marathon (Graydon 1983). Not surprisingly bodies like the WSF which are trying to tackle some of the roots of male chauvinism in sport are underfunded and desperately short of money. Sponsorship in sport of the commercial kind is heavily oriented towards male sport, and in areas where female sport is sponsored it is frequently to a much lower degree than male sport, and sponsored prizes for women in games like tennis are nearly always smaller than the equivalents for male players.

6. Making sport female

It can be seen then that the issue of women and sport is, in the same way as women and leisure generally, a far more complicated problem than at first might appear. Sport, like leisure, has always been male-defined, for men and by men, and it is supported not only by the structures and ideologies of male power within sport itself, but also by patriarchal relations in the household, community and economy. Women can be encouraged, subject to all kinds of caveats to do with class and ethnicity, to take up sport by involving existing non-sporting organizations, (women's organizations, playgroups etc.) or using places where women already go for other reasons (health centres, schools) and by providing things not previously provided, like low fees or a creche. But they will not remain in sport, or see it as an important part of their leisure, unless men's attitudes to women in sport and the home change and unless women can begin to permeate the power and decision making spheres of sport. But this is unlikely to happen without a major struggle, because the sporting activities of many men depend on the services provided by women (from cooking Sunday lunch so a morning male football match is able to go ahead unfettered by domestic responsibilities, to washing sports kit and giving verbal and emotional encouragement to sportsmen). If women start to see sport as something which does not largely exclude them, then men will find it more difficult to get the same levels of support they have previously enjoyed. In competitive sport, as the gap between women's and men's performances continues to decrease, (Owen and Lustig 1985; Ferris 1981; Dyer 1982) some men will find themselves beaten by mere women, who are not afraid of looking 'unfeminine' or being thought honorary men. But sport is not only enjoyable and important to women's health – it can also contribute to a higher level of confidence amongst women, provide a sense that their bodies are not merely playthings for the sexual pleasure of men, but able to do activities other than work, and offer a feeling of physical power. 'Sport for All' is certainly much more threatening than the male-dominated Sports Council ever thought when it first dreamt up its campaigning slogan. Nor is sport just a kind of commercial hype or publicly subsidized 'compensation' therapy for the socially disadvantaged, or a capitalist plot to encourage greater consumption, as Clarke and Critcher (1985) seem to be arguing. As Talbot (1981) shows in these two quotes from women sports participants, sport is like most leisure, a form of self expression, but also more importantly, unlike some other types of leisure, an activity which increases women's control over not only their lives but also over their body and physical strength;

Debbie Brill; I high jump because it is an expression of me . . . It gives me a great sense of my body and mind. When I clear the bar I have a great sense of control and accomplishment.

Swimming was my passion and I gave it all. Letting loose with all of me. An effortless fish, finning forever to a rhythm of breathing and stroking across the pool, a healthy, powerful, well disciplined body that could take me anywhere . . . a natural high so few women have ever experienced. (Quoted in Talbot, 1981, pp 45–45)

Chapter Four; Notes

1. The Women's Sports Foundation is a voluntary body which welcomes individual members and can be contacted at;
   Centre for G.E.S.,
   51 Broomgrove Road, Sheffield, S10.

CHAPTER FIVE

Leisure and the household

1. Home leisure - the peaceful haven?

Leisure which takes place in the community is, as we have seen, affected by many constraints and difficulties for the majority of women, although some are better equipped than others, for a variety of reasons, to overcome those constraints. Leisure in the home however, might be seen in a rather different light, where perhaps some of the constraints influencing women's degree of participation in outside-the-home leisure do not apply-no public spaces need to be traversed, domestic obligations whilst close at hand need not prevent all leisure, less time is needed for home-based leisure and probably less money too. However to believe that home based leisure is straightforward for other than single women living alone (and in this case also there remain problems-obscene phonecalls, fear of the house being broken into, social isolation . . .) is to misunderstand the nature of the constraining factors on women's leisure.

The power of men over women is not confined to situations, relationships and contexts outside the household, but is a crucial part of most women's daily lives inside their homes. Disputes over who does domestic work and childcare and conflicts over who may go outside the home and for what reason are widespread and are extensively documented in the literature on housework (Maynard 1985, Malos 1980, Delphy 1984) and in research on violence in the home (Pahl, J. 1985, Dobash and Dobash 1980). Hence while for men the home may provide a 'peaceful haven', it cannot be guaranteed to offer the same to women.

The home for most women, employed or not, is a workplace in a way that is true for few men, except those that do paid work from home and even in this case it is not the same thing as being a place for unpaid work. Workplaces do not convert easily into places for leisure. Especially for women who are at home all day, undone domestic chores and other aspects of housework are omnipresent.

They cannot escape dirty dishes, grubby carpets and piles of dirty washing by going out of the door and escaping to another workplace as can many men; women with jobs often speak of the pleasure they take as did this one; 'in closing the door behind me when I go off to work where I can't see the dust or worry about the clutter' (school meals worker with two children, Sample B, Milton Keynes study).

All members of a household are likely to see the home as a base for some leisure, but in order to make this possible it is often necessary for women to forfeit their leisure. The continued presence of household duties and obligations means that it is difficult for women to set aside time for leisure at times when others are relaxing which they can be sure will be uninterrupted. It is rare for women who live with others to have a space of their own for leisure, whereas men and frequently children too if they do not simply leave the house, often have special places to go even in cramped housing conditions – a room, a corner of the garden, a shed – where they are likely to remain undisturbed. Home-based leisure too, does not just involve those people who live in a particular household, but often involves other people, friends, acquaintances, relatives, coming into the house. Women may have little or no control over who their male partners bring to the house and indeed may have to sacrifice yet more time catering (often literally) for the needs of such visitors. Consequently women's home based leisure and enjoyment is often based on or derives from, the same activities and tasks which form part of their work in the household, or is fitted into those tasks and activities, sometimes simultaneously. Whilst men's leisure may also derive from work, it is usually from their paid rather than unpaid work and they are from the available evidence, much less likely to combine work and leisure activities simultaneously (how many men iron whilst watching TV or try to read a book whilst cooking the evening meal?). When the home is also a work place it is much more difficult to switch off from things which have to be done, to things which are chosen in their own right – you cannot easily shut up the kitchen or the undusted bedrooms or pretend that bored or hungry children are not there.

So leisure in the home is far from the idyll that some commentators (usually male) believe it to be and has to be fought for and struggled over by women in the same ways that leisure in the community has to be struggled over. No wonder then that much of women's household leisure consists of needlework, knitting, cooking, reading, TV watching, writing letters, day dreaming and snatching quick naps. All of these activities can be fitted into a fragmented time schedule, don't require large blocks of time, are cheap or free, require little space or equipment and can quickly be disposed of or stopped when work obligations intervene. Although as I shall argue in the next chapter, employment is a crucial variable in women's leisure, nevertheless within the home, almost all women whether old or young, with dependent children or adults are not, working or middle class, from an ethnic minority group or majority group, are subject to constraints and determinants on their leisure. These relate partly to male patriarchal power over women. As well as those constraints and determinants, there are further ones which result from living in a capitalist society, which is for example more interested in making a profit out of building houses than whether those houses provided a pleasurable and well-designed leisure and work environment for the people who live in them. Capitalism also invades the home in the form of consumerism; leisure at home often only *seems* private and uncommercialized (e.g. TV, video, records).

2. At-home leisure activities and perceptions of leisure

The problem of what is defined as leisure does not disappear in the home, nor is it an academic problem only–women themselves may find it difficult to decide what aspects of their lives at home are leisure, which are enjoyable through work, and which are definitely work and this has consequences for how and when they are able to relax. Men whose main employment is outside the home seem to have no such problems distinguishing between work, work related activities and obligations, and enjoyment and relaxation, nor do these categories often seem to overlap (Parker, S.R. 1971, 1976). For women, however, the same activities and/or time periods may simultaneously provide both work and leisure. The context or degree of choice which enters into whether something is done or not can also help to determine whether it is seen as leisure or not. So ironing, which is mostly not seen as enjoyable, may enable some leisure because it can be combined with watching TV. Whilst cooking dinner for the household is not either seen as enjoyable or leisure, cooking a meal for friends can be both and is not regarded as work. Other activities which many women did, for example in the Milton Keynes study, such as writing letters, may not be regarded as leisure because they aren't seen as important or legitimate uses of time by other people in the household: letter-writing may also involve tasks (condolences, thank-yous) others won't undertake. Women who are in employment do seem, from the Milton Keynes research at least, more able to compartmentalize their time than women who are involved only in unpaid work, and thus exercise more control over their lives and perceive their leisure in a different way from women whose ability to control their lives are lessened by total financial dependence on a male income and whose unpaid work is not easily or at all compartmentalized.

The 1983 General Household Survey data on leisure activities (*Social Trends* 1985) offers the gender related breakdown of home-based activities as seen in Table 5.1.

TABLE 5.1   Home-based activities by gender, Great Britain 1983

Percentages in each group engaging in each activity in four weeks before interview	males	females
activity	%	%
listening to records and tapes	65	62
gardening	50	39
needlework, knitting	2	48
house repairs and DIY	51	24
reading books	50	61

SOURCE: Table 10.3 *Social Trends* 1985, p. 149

But of course this kind of data does not necessarily tell us whether all the DIY and gardening done by these individuals was enjoyable, nor whether some undertook these activities purely as work. *Social Trends* also tells us that women watch television more than men, according to research by the BBC in 1983–4, with women watching nearly four hours more than men a week in the first quarter of 1984, and nearly three hours more than men in the summer months. Women are less likely to read a daily newspaper than men but more likely to read weekly magazines (in 1983 46 per cent of women read a women's weekly magazine, *Social Trends* 1985). None of this information gives us any indication of the amount of time nor the *quality* of time that women are able to devote to these various activities. Also the GHS data is derived from prompted responses (that is, interviewees are offered certain activities and asked if they do them) which as a method is far from satisfactory. Nor of course does it tell us anything about the conditions under which home-based leisure takes place.

If we turn to the more detailed studies on women however there is only a slightly greater variety of activities evident, although these are subject to all kinds of variation, including seasonality, ethnicity, social class, life cycle differences and household size. In the Milton Keynes study TV was the most popular home-based activity amongst Study A women, followed by sewing and embroidery, gardening and care of houseplants, knitting, reading and listening to the radio. In the Milton Keynes sample B, popular at-home activities during the day were reading, 'just relaxing', sitting down, watching TV, knitting, sewing, radio, sleeping and gardening. Unlike the GHS, none of these were prompted responses. Evening activities at home mostly consisted of TV and sitting down quietly when there was nothing pressing to do. But evenings, as the last chapter suggested, are often a busy time for women at home and such relaxation as did occur was often fleeting for the women in the Milton Keynes study. Where longer time-periods were available there was a clear preference for going out as this removed the likelihood that leisure would be interrupted by household tasks. I also asked in Study B what aspects of daily routine women found pleasurable and here playing with children emerged as an important part of pleasure in everyday life, alongside the more ubiquitous TV, reading, gardening, and relaxing, with cooking being a significant minority choice when it took the form of baking, jam making or any cookery *not* involving routine meal preparation.

In the Sheffield NOP study TV, knitting, sewing and other crafts plus reading, and sitting down 'doing nothing' were major evening and week day activities, with a preference for weekend activities to be out-of-home rather than in home, with the exception of TV viewing (Green, Hebron and Woodward 1985b). The Sheffield study also suggests that there are social class variations discernible in the pattern discovered, with middle class women more likely to enjoy gardening and less likely to watch TV, and working class women doing more TV watching than reading. Working class women, older women and those with dependent children were also more likely to spend evenings relaxing or doing nothing (Green, Hebron and Woodward, 1985b). The Leeds study of Armley suggested that leisure for women there was about 'being with people, watching television, reading, drinking and playing bingo' (Dixey and Talbot, 1982 p.61). The weekly evening time-tables of women of different backgrounds in this study reveal similar choices of at-home leisure to the Milton Keynes and Sheffield studies, although there are evident life cycle variations in the amount of leisure time spent on home-based leisure rather than out-of-home leisure. Wimbush's (1985) Scottish research on well-being indicates that at-home leisure is often spent alone, with some encouragement of partners and children to go out, thus making solitude possible. On the other hand, Talbot and Dixey (1982) found that women whose husbands were frequently absent from the house because of leisure involvement, rationalized this situation by developing their own home-based interests and were therefore able to contain any resentment they might otherwise have at their partners being out frequently. But Wimbush's (1985) research is worth pausing over because it stresses the extent to which what is done at home reflects the state of health and energy (or its absence) of individual women. Often tiredness limits the range of things done in the home, especially in the evenings, which may explain the lack of variation in the kinds of leisure women have at home. The Sheffield study findings confirm this view too. One of Hunt's (1980) respondents in her study of a Staffordshire mining village sums up this tiredness and its effects thus:

> Alan doesn't come in 'till twenty past or half past six at night. So by the time we've had tea we haven't got time to go out very far. We don't go out much. We watch the television and I do a bit of reading. *Women* and *Women's Own*, and I knit in between when I feel like it. Quarter past nine I feel that tired, I always have an hour and then my Ovaltine and go to bed. (Carol Parker, in Hunt 1980, pp. 49–50)

The lack of variety is not the only feature of home-based leisure for women. Whilst a high proportion of home-based activities or leisure involve a certain and very understandable degree of passivity (sitting down, TV, radio, cat-naps) which insofar as they are allowed to be uninterrupted are often a necessary recuperative strategy, others including gardening, sewing, knitting and embroidery actually involve production and creativity. As Delphy (1984) points out, much of what is done in the household, but not remunerated, involves production as well as consumption, and indeed this applies to leisure as much as to housework (or as Delphy prefers to call it, familial work). Nor is it always the case that what is produced by home-based leisure is for the the benefit of the woman herself, although it *may* be in the case of dressmaking or sewing.

More often however it is others in the family who are recipients of things produced by women in their leisure time – garments, household items, a pleasant garden or beautiful houseplants, a cake. Just as Thompson (1983) talks about the ways in which doing something creative in the form of adult education appeals to women, so does the same notion appeal to many women in the home. But this latter 'choice' is limited by many factors including the kinds of craft skills easily available to women in school, further and adult education, and the costs of materials and the way these are marketed, as well as available space and whether others in a household see these activities as a legitimate use of time.

3. Who does what in the household and how long does it take?

At one level this is a simple and easily answered question, but at another level it is extremely complicated because there is no straightforward definition of what constitutes household work. A lot of the current debates over the 'informal economy' (that is, the economy outside the formal one – casual work, DIY, voluntary work etc) have considered this question, but provided no more sophisticated answers than previously (see Finnegan, 1985 and Pahl R. 1985. Pahl (R) talks of the various strategies adopted by households with regard to the work to be done and distinguishes between formal employment, informal employment (i.e. work for those *outside* the household, for example mending a friend's car or baking a cake for a friend) and communal/household work. But he found that the last two categories in particular presented great difficulties of definition, with the result that his Isle of Sheppey research concentrated on 'the labour that is done *for* households, including whether or not they do it themselves' (Pahl, R. 1985, p. 213). Thus he drew up a list of forty one tasks ranging from house maintenance, home improvement and routine housework to producton, car maintenance and child-care. It was found that much of this work was done by the household and was not paid for, with house improvement and house extension tasks being those most frequently done and paid for in the formal market sector. Pahl also attempted a highly complicated system for exploring the division of labour between household partners. This included weighting according to whether the tasks were in practice and to what extent they are conventionally, male or female and how frequently a task is done (for example painting may be done bi-annually, making beer less that once every four months, cooking two or three times daily). Pahl's analysis of the Isle of Sheppey material, after all this, still allows him to say little more than that 'it is overwhelmingly obvious that women do most of the work in the household . . . the domestic division of labour is more unequally shared by women . . . they also do substantial *amounts* . . . there is very little variation between the classes' (Pahl, R. 1985, p. 270–272). However Pahl did find that the employment status of women and their age far outweighed the importance of social class factors in determining the domestic division of labour, with the most assymetrical division of labour occuring when women are not in employment and have young children. Hunt's smaller ethnographic study (1980) is able to reach the same conclusion in a rather less obtuse way, but both Pahl and Hunt have done very relevant work which is not necessarily seen as being about leisure at all.

What such studies as these tell us is about the limited amount of time many women have available in the home for leisure, something which both my own research and the Sheffield study confirm, which helps to explain why women's at-home-leisure activities are either those which are linked to domestic work, or are things which require no advanced preparation and can be done in short time-spells.

Green, Hebron and Woodward (1985b) found in the Sheffield study that whilst most women in the NOP survey said that they had between two and four hours free every weekday evening, 15 per cent had under one hour per evening. Women with dependent children were found to have less free time that those without, and women under 25 and over 45 (those *least* likely to have dependent children) have most free time. Similar patterns (varying with age and dependants) were also found to be the case for weekend free-time, with 65 per cent of women having five or more hours of free time, but women with dependent children having least.

Time budget studies also offer some insights into the tasks women have to do and the amount of time left over, although as Pahl, R. (1985) and Wyatt (1985) have pointed out, time budget studies do have limitations, not least of which is a failure on the part of respondents to include simultaneous activities in their time diaries and failure to record some activities at all. Time budget studies prior to 1975 show that although the amount of domestic work was decreasing over the post-war decades, women were still doing most of the work, and as Pahl R. (1985) says of these studies, 'while men are doing more non-routine work in terms of domestic maintenance and improvement, their contribution to the routine domestic tasks is still in the order of 'helping' rather than any substantial shift to true role reversal.' (Pahl, R. 1985, p. III). Maynard (1985) says also that 'More recent research shows women spending amounts of time on domestic tasks, to the extent that if it was paid employment it would certainly be regarded as full time (Berk and Berk, 1979)' (Maynard 1985, p. 81). All the time budget data suggests that the longest working week of any person is that of employed women, even though their absence outside the home ensures that they do fewer hours of housework than non-employed women. Finch's (1983b) perceptive study of the incorporation of women into their husbands' jobs, offers a nice illustration of this in the following extract from the diary of the wife of a clergyman, who (unusually for a cleric's wife) had a full-time job as a primary school teacher;

Day: Monday
  Got up at: 7.30

Morning:
  7.30 to 8.30   Prepared husband's lunch and pre-set it in cooker.
                      Breakfast
  8.30 to 12.00   At school
  Lunch at 12.30   On duty

Afternoon:

1.00 to 4.00	At school
4.00 to 4.30	Cup of tea and crossword
4.30 to 5.30	Cleaned landing and stairs and washed down all the paint work. Prepared tea.

Evening meal at: 6.00

Evening:

7.00 to 9.30	Weekly ironing
9.30 to 10.30	Watched TV and discussed church cleaning for tomorrow

Went to bed at   11.00

(Finch, 1983b, p. 56–7)

This woman's free time thus consisted of half an hour after finishing teaching, and one hour much later in the evening, with the latter being interrupted by having also to discuss something connected with her husband's (but not her) job. For many women in similar situations, this is an all too familiar scene. As Delphy (1985) argues, the problem of housework is not exhausted by looking at the tasks and duties which it consists of; it is 'a certain *work relationship,* a particular relationship of production, it is all the work done unpaid for others within the confines of the household' (Delphy, 1985, p. 90). Time budget studies can tell us about the tasks it involves, and something about the time that is thus taken up, but they offer only a limited insight into the kinds of relationships between women and men which underlie that work and time division. I do not want at this point to get into the debates which Delphy and others are engaged in about who benefits from women's household work, but whether it is men alone or capitalism alone or both, there is no doubt that women themselves benefit little and that the necessity to do household work quite dramatically affects women's free time and their leisure.

The task, time and complicated relationships inplicated in household work increases still further when a household contains dependent children (Maynard, 1985) or sick or disabled adult dependents (Finch and Groves, 1983). As Berk and Berk (1979) show, although male partners do get involved in childcare, this is often the more pleasant tasks such as playing, rather than nappy changing or feeding or washing. Where men are significantly involved in the more mundane aspects of childcare, it is often because they are unemployed or are middle class fathers with professional jobs, flexible hours and a political commitment to gender equality in the household (O'Brien, 1982, Russell 1983, Hunt 1980). But for women, childcare is double edged anyway – it both prevents them from having leisure or much leisure, and is a source of enjoyment in itself, both in terms of children's play and company (Green *et al.* 1985b; Milton Keynes study B). Also, as one woman in the Dixey and Talbot (1982) study said, 'Children help you discover all sorts of things. You wouldn't dream of going out and putting a pair of ice-skates on but when you've got children with you you don't think twice about it' (Dixey and Talbot, 1982, p. 60). Adult dependents such as ageing relatives or a sick or handicapped husband however are much more likely to destroy leisure than to provide it, especially since such 'caring' work is seen to be properly the task of women. As Ungerson (1983) demonstrates, the nature of caring for the sick, mentally-ill and disabled and the time this takes are extremely demanding and usually undertaken by females alone. Where it is a handicapped child that requires care, Ungerson's material suggests fathers may help with tasks like lifting, but not with washing, feeding or nappy-changing.

Time, tasks and the nature of the relationships underlying caring and housework then can be seen to be significant constraints on the leisure of many women, although there are of course life cycle variations in this.

4. Household routines and leisure

One of the arguments that used to be used by sociologists of leisure about housewives was that as they were largely responsible for organizing their own day's work, they therefore had more freedom than others (i.e. those in paid employment) for organizing their work and leisure (Parker 1971). This argument has also surfaced again more recently (Gregory 1982). Such arguments ignore the extent to which housework and childcare are actually organized around and made necessary by sets of power relationships, principally those between men and women. As Delphy (1985) points out, there is a big difference between the work which an individual does to sustain themselves in their household and the work which is necessary to sustain others. The former is not really housework or familial work but the latter is, and is made more difficult by the fact that it then has to satisfy others' demands and ideas about how it should be done. Thus while a young single woman living alone can decide for herself whether to dust or hoover the carpet, a woman with a male partner and children, especially if she is financially dependent on the man, has also to take into consideration the effects on those other household members and on herself if she does not carry out certain tasks.

Dixey and Talbot (1982) argue that whilst women are aware that there is some degree 'in practice' of autonomy involved in housework, in fact they rarely make use of this (that is, the power relationships and ideologies surrounding it are influential). In addition to setting their own standards (the Leeds study found women who preferred to wash by hand even though they had washing machines because they felt hand washing got clothes cleaner), 'housewives are reminded each day of the standards they are expected to reach. If not from husbands and children, from the television, magazines, hoardings and from other women; housewives are bombarded with images of standards which they cannot reach.' (Dixey and Talbot, 1982, p. 23). These standards often involve setting up weekly and monthly lists of tasks and organizing some aspects of housework round a routine which though it may frequently be broken by children or by husbands' unexpected arrivals, departures or demands, is rarely broken for reasons to do with women's personal leisure. Not only this, but the nature of housework is that much of it is repetitive and one done soon needs redoing; this is *untrue* of many of the activities Pahl, R. (1985) defines as household work:

> sometimes I will get finished early, before the kids get home, and I'll sit down in the front room with a magazine – but then I'd often start looking at the nets or the carpet and think – maybe I should have washed the nets or hoovered round again – more often than not having thought of it I put down my book and go and do it (woman with three children, Milton Keynes study B, no paid employment)

In the Milton Keynes research I found that women with no paid employment and who claimed not to be currently seeking a job (a category I am aware is problematic and to which I will return in the next chapter) were the most likely to have organized their housework into a routine, which both structured their day and possibly allowed them a small amount of space for themselves. Women with jobs had less need for a routine in the house because they already had a more immutable structure provided by the times during which they were at their jobs, and housework as well as leisure had to be fitted into what was left over. The Sheffield study found that almost half the women interviewed in the NOP survey had no free time during the day at all (weekends excepted) and that the likelihood of this was greatest (not least) amongst those *in employment*. Those who did have free time said they took it when they could, rather than trying to plan it in advance. But having free time and feeling able to use it *as you wish* are not the same, and even those women who do have time available to them in the day may only use it for certain kinds of activities, involving either their own homes or the homes of friends and relatives, rather than out-of-home leisure.

Women do not, as I have already indicated, act as free agents in determining their own routines when they live in households with men and or children. Even where they live alone, the ideologies of marriage and female roles are still influential. Men's jobs and leisure interests were a significant determinant of what women were able to do in their nonwork time in the Milton Keynes study, influencing when and whether leisure was possible on a regular and predictable basis. As Finch (1983b) shows, some male jobs (including self-employment) are so all-encompassing both of their encumbent and his wife that very little in the way of leisure may be planned by the women concerned. Certain kinds of jobs, for instance those of the clergy, armed forces and police may even determine who women may make friends with and who not. Shift work or work which involves long periods of time away from home (oilrig workers, those with jobs abroad, merchant seamen etc.) can also seriously disrupt women's free time and cause radical rearrangements of the time spent and what is involved in doing housework. Children's school hours and out-of-school activities may also have the same effect. But it is not only the appearance or absence of others in the household at particular times which affects women; it is also their presence. Studies of unemployed men suggest that one source of strain is that women used to being at home all day on their own find it hard to get used to having men around too (Burgoyne 1985, and Fagin and Little, 1984) because this destroys not only their routine but also even the illusion of autonomy. Murcott (1983) has also drawn attention to the ways in which men's expectations about meals and women's own ideas about 'a proper meal' in South Wales (i.e. 'meat and veg', not beans on toast or fish and chips) may also influence what women expect to do in the way of cooking and how long this will take them. Employed working class men in manual jobs are expected to require, and indeed expect themselves, a substantial meal at least once a day. Delphy (1985) notes this tendency in French peasant families where men also have to have the best cut of meat or the largest portion and significant attention is paid to preparing their meal. Cooking 'proper' meals takes time and usually has to be set into a routine which takes into account a man's working hours (which may be variable or unsocial) and shopping as well as preparation.

Ideologies about female gender roles and marriage, as well as the power relations of households and the structures of family life, are very influential on women's at-home leisure. Household routines and their structuring around other household members, are also a significant factor shaping what leisure time a woman has available to her, when and the quality of that time. Although much housework is predictable and repetitive, in households of several people there are always likely to be contingencies which upset or alter any routine which has been established. It is this unpredictability and fragmentation which women (especially those without paid employment of their own which can form time boundaries around which they are not available for housework) may find difficult to manage in terms of setting aside time where they are able to choose what to do or whether to do anything at all, quite apart from the extent to which women's leisure is seen by the rest of the household as at all legitimate.

5. Money and household budgeting

This is a topic which is important both for in-home leisure and leisure in the community insofar as leisure involves spending money. But it is also important because it provides one indice of the distribution of power in households. Home leisure is made possible by negotiating household power relations, including financial power. As Hunt (1980) says, 'the *way* a family handles money tells us a considerable amount about the nature of the relationships prevailing in that household' (Hunt, 1980, p. 37–8). In addition there are, as Hunt's material shows, contradictions between what is *thought* to happen in the distribution of a family's income and what happens in practice. One of her respondents, Maureen Clark, manages her family finances and she and her husband have a joint account, but this does not give both partners equal freedom to draw on the money;

> When I was working I bought a lot of clothes, shoes, handbags and hats. Of course I don't have the same amount of money now . . . I think nothing of going out and spending £7.50 on a shirt for my husband if I like it, but I would think, 'I should have to buy myself two jumpers and two blouses for that money'. (Hunt, 1980, pp. 38–9).

Later discussions with the same woman suggested to Hunt that this restraint was imposed as much by Maureen's husband and his views on what his wife should spend money, as by Maureen herself.

Hunt notes in her study the tendency on the behalf of men, whatever the household budgeting system, to keep back some money for their personal spending in a way not possible for non-earing wives. A similar tendency was noted by Bell and McKee (1984) in their study of the domestic and marital consequences of male unemployment, where men in receipt of benefits still kept back some money for themselves. One wife said:

> He thinks when he got £150 he'd want a bit of it and I have the rest. And he seems to think it's me who's having it, but it's not me. I spend it on paying the bills, buying food, clothes, things like that. But he seems to get the idea it's me who's having it. Whereas with

him, when he has his cut, it's being spent on him. (Bell and McKee, 1984, p. 21).

Research by Gray (1979) in Edinburgh indicated that in families with a very rigid housekeeping system, women were more likely to enter paid employment partly so that they had some measure of financial control. Households where men gave women a fixed sum of housekeeping each week were mostly those where the male was in unskilled and physically fatiguing employment. Giving a fixed sum allowed any overtime pay to be concealed from wives and also offered a clear measure of masculine financial control.

Pahl, J. (1982) has commented that there is an important distinction to be made between control of money (which refers to the point where money enters the household), management of money, which concerns the system of allocation within a household, and budgeting which is about spending on different categories of items and services. She suggests that there are at least four different allocative systems although empirically it isn't always that clearcut. First is the whole wage system, in which one partner, usually the woman, manages all the household's finances, but where the personal spending money of the other partner is taken out before the wage packet is handed over. If both partners earn, then both sets of wages are managed by one person. If it is the man who manages the finances, the woman may have no personal spending money of her own at all. The second is the allowance system where the man gives the woman a set amount and she has to pay for particular items of household expenditure. The rest of the money is retained by the male partner who pays for other specific items. If a woman has no earnings of her own under this system then she has no personal money. The third is the shared management system where both partners have access to all the household money and both manage it. Personal spending money is taken out of the pool. The fourth system is the independent management system where both partners have an income and neither has access to all the household's money; each partner takes responsibility for specific items of expenditure, but retains independent control over their own money.

In fieldwork in East Kent, Pahl, J. (1985) found that the majority of households used the pooling system, with about one fifth using the allowance system. Pahl and other researchers note that there is a crucial tie-up between money allocation systems and the balance of power in the household, with women having least power where they have neither a pooling or independent management system, nor wages of their own. Most researchers also report that money is the subject which respondents are least willing to talk about, which is possibly an indication of the importance it has within private household power-relations. (Hunt, 1980).

In the Sheffield study, Green, Hebron and Woodward (1985b) found that about half the NOP sample said leisure spending comes from joint money, 41 per cent said it was from their partner, 7 per cent got it from their own money and only 1 per cent from housekeeping. Women with full-time jobs, those with no children and young women were most likely to have access to joint money. The amount actually spent on leisure per week varied from nothing to over £20, but nearly half the sample spent between £2 and £10 weekly. In the Milton Keynes sample B, I asked how women would pay for any new leisure activity and found that one quarter said they wouldn't be able to afford one as they had no personal money, 28.5 per cent said it would come from their own income and 26 per cent said it would come from a joint income. Those most able to afford something new were in full-time jobs, and those least likely were unemployed women or those from households where their partner was unemployed. Money itself is clearly important because even in-home activities often cost money, whether it is for extra heating, knitting-wool or flour, margarine and eggs for cake baking. Money is one of the indices of who is in control of their lives and choices, and who is not; it offers insights into the distribution of power and authority in a household by suggesting where power to control expenditure lies. Women who have little or no financial power may also have little control over their time, work and leisure.

6. Homes as places for leisure

It has already been suggested that there are many reasons why women are likely to have at-home leisure. It is usually cheaper, easier and requires no travel or transport; at-home activities or interests can be more easily adjusted than out-of-home ones to fit the requirements of domestic obligations, child care commitments and the needs of other dependants, and there are likely to be fewer objections from male partners, especially if that leisure takes place when they are out. But as Glyptis and Chambers (1982) pointed out when embarking on their ESRC/Sports Council sponsored 'Leisure in the Home' project, the home

> must accommodate individual and communal activity, and perhaps several activities simultaneously for different members of the household . . . Few people have the luxury of designing or fitting a home principally with leisure needs in mind . . . But the leisure opportunities and constraints posed by the physical characteristics of the home and its immediate surroundings must critically affect the quality of leisure of its occupants. (Glyptis and Chambers, 1982, pp. 247–8).

They suggest that there are a number of attributes of homes which affect leisure, including size, division of space into indoor and outdoor, design (layout and access to rooms, as well as competing uses of space), flexibility, and the way space is managed by the household. For most women the only space (in other than single households) which is likely to be given over to them is the kitchen, which at busy times of the day is likely to offer anything but a peaceful haven and whose design is often oriented to servicing a household rather than towards providing privacy and a basis for leisure.

My Milton Keynes in-depth interview data (I did not ask anything similar on the questionnaires) suggested that even where households were living in small houses (in Milton Keynes these are mostly privately built rather than rental houses which despite some other disadvantages, have tended to be spacious) men and children often had some space they could call their own – a bedroom, shed, allotment, corner of the garden or garage, or in middle class households even a study, but that women rarely had such a space. Kitchens, as I have already suggested, whilst often occupied by women, do not provide privacy or solitude quite apart from the other disadvantages associated with being in a place designed for and used as a work-base. Cookery and listening to the radio apart, there are few solitary, leisure activities which are happily located in a kitchen unless it is exceptionally large. Partly this is because the kitchen is an ever-present reminder of undone chores. Although women who are at home during the day in a household where other members are out at work or school theoretically have access to the whole of their home during that time, during winter or cold weather this may be of little use if the rooms thus available are cold and unheated. Several women in the course of my interviews said that although their house had central heating, reasons of economy (sometimes imposed by male partners safely out of freezing cold homes during the day and so unaware of the consequences) dictated turning off the heating during the day. Gardens are an important leisure space for some women and may provide at certain times of the day or week a private place, but this is seasonal and also subject to invasion by others at certain times (weekends, school holidays etc.). Gardens may also accommodate work (e.g. washing) or represent work for those women who hate gardening.

The home also stores and contains as Glyptis and Chambers (1982) note, various forms of leisure equipment (the nature of which is mainly dictated by commercial concerns) for members of the household, but the leisure equipment most women use certainly appears from the Milton Keynes, Sheffield and Leeds studies to be fairly limited in extent, is acquired primarily for its work-related usefulness–sewing machines, baking tins, knitting machines–or is something all the household has access to (television, radio, hi-fi). In the case of the latter there are often bitter disputes over who should use it and what should be viewed or listened to. Homes as leisure bases for women thus tend to have severe disadvantages relating to their dual work leisure use, the presence of other household members and lack of privacy.

Leisure in the home

This chapter has tried to explore both the kinds of leisure activities (or non-activities) which women pursue in the home, and those processes and constraints which are based on the household and affect all leisure, not just that which is home-based. The fact that much of women's leisure at particular stages in the life cycle (especially mothers of dependent children and women over sixty) takes place in the home cannot automatically be assumed to mean that women are quite satisfied with that state of affairs, although some of them clearly are. Nor is the home necessarily the kind of peaceful haven for women that it is often presumed to provide for other family members. Not only is the home a workplace for most women, whether in employment or not, but it is also the site of conflictual power relationships between men, women and children. Women's role in the home is also shaped by powerful ideologies about marriage and gender. Women whose leisure takes place in the home are not at risk from sexual assault or harassment whilst travelling to leisure activities, but are still at risk from sexual assault, rape and other forms of violence from men whilst they are at home. (Pahl, J. 1985a, Brownmiller 1975, Hanmer and Maynard 1986). Money (and struggles over it) is less important for home-based activities than it is for leisure outside the home, but it is still a relevant consideration and influences how much status, confidence and power women have. Pahl (R., 1985) found that the unemployed aren't able to use the informal economy as a compensation for not being employed in the formal economy, because they can't afford the necessary equipment and materials. The leisure of others in the household also takes place in the home or is fought out in the household, and the leisure of males and children can and often does, take precedence over the leisure of women. Women's leisure does not seem to command the same degree of legitimacy as men's leisure, either in the home or out of it and whether we are talking about time, space, money or resources. Leisure in the home is affected by many factors external to the home, including employment, working hours, school hours and terms, social structure and cultural ideological beliefs about what is acceptable. Capitalism dictates how houses are designed and what leisure equipment is available. For women from certain ethnic minority groups cultural factors may result in them being even more confined to home-based leisure than other women (for example Asian small-shop owners); it is significant that ethnicity is something missing from most of the existing research on women's leisure and is partly related to the invisibility of women from some ethnic minority groups. But there are also many other things which we do not know about women's leisure in the home and which are not easily accessible to us, either through interviews or diary-based budget studies. The trend towards privatization of family life originally noted by sociologists in the 1960s and 1970s does not seem to have decreased, but many of the implications and processes of that privatization are actually hidden from view. Almost no studies of female leisure for instance, mention sexual activity. But it is not apparent whether this is because women don't want to talk about their sex lives (some researchers looking at more general family life have not found this problem, Holly 1985) or because women don't think of sexual activity as leisure. Whilst it is possible to pick out certain categories of women whose at-home leisure seems more varied or more facilitated than others, (those without young children, single women, women with co-operative partners and children, women with high incomes and large houses) it is not yet possible to say, other than on the basis of region-specific studies, which combinations of social and economic factors are most or least likely to provide women with leisure. It may be that the patterning is more random than we might suppose, or that it is possible to do something about improving the home-based leisure of many women only in conjunction with very far reaching and radical changes in the organization of our society; certainly what we know so far suggests the latter.

In the next chapter I shall turn my attention to the relationship between employment and leisure, exploring in particular the extent to which women without employment may be disadvantaged *vis-a-vis* employed women in their leisure time, enjoyment, perceptions and range of activities.

CHAPTER SIX

Employment, unemployment and leisure

1. Leisure employment and the gender model

So far I have been concentrating on the kinds of leisure women have, the contexts of that leisure and some of the constraints which operate to restrict the range of experiences and time available to women for their leisure. In this chapter I want to continue to explore some of those issues, but want to do so by examining the interrelationships between leisure and whether or not women are in employment. In so doing I will also be referring to the effects on women's leisure of male employment and unemployment, but the principal concern is the influences on leisure of women themselves being in or out of paid employment. A great deal of empirical work has been done on the relationship between male employment and leisure (Parker, 1971, 1976; Roberts 1981) and it has also been the subject of some sophisticated theoretical and historical work (Thompson, 1967, Burns 1973). But although there has in recent years been an explosion of work on women's employment and unemployment *per se* (see Dex, 1985) much of this has been concerned primarily with either the nature of the jobs done by women and the effects of women's employment and redundancy on their domestic lives, or has looked at the processes and structures through which male patriarchal control over women is exercised by men in the workplace. A few studies have however tried to look at women's lives as a whole in the context of paid employment or job loss (Coyle, 1984, Westwood, 1984).

A great deal of the research done on employed women has adopted what Feldberg and Glenn (1984) call a 'gender model' of explanation as opposed to what the same authors call a 'Job Model' which is the standard explanatory tool used to account for male employment behaviour and attitudes. That is, the job model explains all, *not* just employment-specific behaviour, in terms of the working conditions and types of jobs done, whereas the 'gender model' disregards the characteristics of jobs and working conditions, explaining behaviour in terms of personal characteristics and family obligations and tasks. Although there is not yet anything like the same volume of literature on women's leisure as there is on women's employment, the prevalence of the gender model is already apparent, and stands in contrast to the 'job model' which has frequently been the driving force behind explanations of men's leisure. There have been different reasons for this in the field of leisure than in the field of work, mainly related in the case of leisure research to the manner in which women's experience of leisure has the 'gender model' in studies of women's leisure has not had the effect, on the whole, of developing myths about leisure as the 'gender model' has in the study of work (Dex, 1985) except the belief that housewives' lives are pure leisure (Parker 1971).

There is a great danger in explaining the whole of women's experience of leisure in terms *only* of gender. There are, of course, as I have demonstrated in earlier chapters, factors which are important determinants of leisure and which are common to the experience of almost all women (housework for example, or the extent to which women's out-of-home leisure is constrained by fears of sexual assault, rape and harassment, regardless of differences in the lives and situation of different groups of women). But at the same time there are differences *between* women which are as important at dividing them as gender is at giving them a commonality of experience. Failure to take this into account not only results in the neglect of crucial factors such as ethnicity, but further means that everything that has ever been learnt about male or unisex leisure is actually thrown out of the window. In some instances this has been a good thing, but there are points whose significance seems to have been lost altogether. In particular, the argument about the extent to which certain kinds of jobs or even just any job makes it possible for individuals to compartmentalize their days and lives, which in turn allows their leisure time to be fairly clearly demarcated from other aspects of their lives, seems to me to be less irrelevant to women than has been supposed (McIntosh, 1981, Chambers 1985). That is, where women are in paid employment and where their jobs are such that they neither involve doing paid work at home, nor lack clear definition of working hours and tasks/responsibilities, then the impact of that paid employment may make a considerable difference to their leisure, in the same way as it would if they were men. It can provide the possibility of compartmentalizing time and lives in a way which offers some women more clearly defined and better quality leisure than other women. This however doesn't mean that gender is irrelevant, anymore than gender is irrelevant to the employment, leisure and behaviour of men. It simply means we have to take fully into account a range of factors, of which gender is only one dimension. Otherwise we end up in the position of saying that all women, regardless of their economic status, ethnicity, cultural background, attitudes and conditions of existence, all have identical leisure experiences. No study so far has been able to say this on the basis of empirical data.

Employment is clearly of great and increasing importance to women between school leaving age and retirement age. Although it is apparent that some of the growth in women's employment has been amongst middle class married women rather than amongst working class women (who have a long tradition of involvement in paid employment dating from the nineteenth century and before) nevertheless it is the case that the increase in labour force participation by women has been greatest amongst women aged between thirty-five and fifty-four years old. However it is as Dex (1985) points out, important to realize that this increase in employed women over the period since the Second World War (from 27 per cent of the workforce in 1881 and 33.6 per cent in 1948 to 41.7 per cent in 1980) may represent not so much a change in marriage relationships and expectations as a change in child-rearing practices. As the recent national study of employed women by Martin and Roberts (1984) for the Department of Employment shows, not only have attitudes towards married women working changed and liberalized, but so too have the employment histories of women – the gaps left between jobs for childbirth and childrearing are getting shorter (with women also returning to work between births too) and some women are not having any employment break at all for children except statutory maternity leave (although the latter is still very much a minority choice mainly related to lack of childcare provision). Women are also on average having fewer children than in earlier decades of the century. But there are also other dimensions of the changes which have taken place in women's employment, the most important of which so far as the study of leisure is concerned is that a large proportion of employed women are in part-time jobs (42 per cent of employed women were in part-time jobs in 1981 and between 1961 and 1981 there has been a rise of 2.3 million in the number of part-time jobs). At the same time as these developments, in the period since the 1970s women's unemployment relative to men has been rising, although there is still considerable disagreement over whether women have suffered disproportionately in comparison with unemployed men (Dex 1985). Furthermore we also know that the conditions, labour market position and types of work done by women still in employment tend to differ quite markedly from those of men. Not only is entry to the labour market divided by gender (Garnsey, Rubery and Wilkinson 1985) but there is also vertical and horizontal gender segregations of and between occupations and workplaces (Hakim 1981). Women are heavily concentrated in clerical, semi-skilled factory, domestic and retail selling work, with some 30 per cent of them in clerical jobs. We also know that employed women in Britain who are in full-time jobs are paid considerably less than men (New Earnings Survey 1984) and that women in part-time jobs are disadvantaged relative to full-time employees with respect to not only pay-rates but also holiday pay, sickness and pension benefits, promotion prospects and security of employment (Beechey and Perkins forthcoming, Perkins 1983, Aldred 1981). All these factors and features of employment for women mean that it is impossible to leave out a consideration of the character and conditions of that employment when considering leisure.

This task however is far from straightforward. Whilst it is not usually difficult to establish which women are employed (although women who do home-work or casual work may not want to draw this to the attention of researchers) it is much more difficult to decide whether women are unemployed (Bruegel 1983). When I carried out Study B in the Milton Keynes research I was especially interested in how the experiences of female employment and female/male unemployment affected leisure (Deem 1985). But I soon discovered that it is hard for researchers and women themselves to decide when a woman is unemployed. The problem is slightly easier when the study concerns women who have recently lost their jobs, although even in that situation it isn't straightforward (Martin and Wallace 1984). For women with young children or women approaching retirement the self-definition of themselves as unemployed is likely to be most problematic, since it is on these women that there are the greatest structural and ideological pressures to perceive themselves as neither part of, nor wanting to be part of, the labour force. Women who are married are in general also less likely than men or single women to be in receipt of unemployment or other benefits which may also decrease the chances of them perceiving themselves as unemployed. Martin and Wallace tried in their (1984) study to determine the degree of commitment women had to the idea of market employment, by asking a series of questions about their other roles, expectations of how much of their pre-retirement lives they would expect to spend in employment and about their attitudes towards women holding paid employment. But it is obviously not practicable in a study primarily about leisure to devote so much time to asking about 'market attachment'. Nor are questions about 'seeking employment' likely to yield much useful information (Bruegel 1983 found women looking for jobs who didn't think of themselves as unemployed). Various studies have shown, even amongst women recently made redundant that there are likely to be various responses, only one of which is to get another job (Wood 1981).

There is then no easy solution to this problem but it is important to be aware of it. Women who define themselves as housewives or mothers only are not necessarily, in so doing, defining themselves as completely outside the labour market on a permanent basis (as Bruegel (1983) notes, some women not looking for jobs may still enter employment 'accidentally'). Nor are women who themselves define their situation as unemployed necessarily going to retain that perception over a long period of time, if their circumstances change or if no suitable job can be found. However the way in which people define themselves is of relevance to their lifestyles and behaviour and I shall suggest later that married or co-habiting women who define themselves as unemployed may have different leisure experiences from both those who are employed and those who do not have any regular and significant paid employment, but who define themselves primarily in terms of domestic work roles. At the same time it has to be recognized that the conditions and nature of any job which a woman has can also affect her leisure; low-paid part-time or very physically demanding work is likely to produce a different leisure pattern from full-time and reasonably-paid professional, technical or managerial employment. On top of this have to be added all the caveats about using both the 'job' and the 'gender' models to explain women's leisure. But our present state of knowledge about women and leisure does not really provide detailed enough evidence to say with any degree of certainty just what effects different jobs have on the lives of the women who hold them. All that is possible here therefore is to look at the overall impact on women's leisure of having a job or being without regular paid employment.

2. Employed women and leisure

Employment is something which has both advantages and disadvantages so far as leisure is concerned. Its disadvantages are bound up with lack of time and energy for non-job related activities once other tasks and responsibilities have been accomplished. Thus, as a number of writers have argued, employed women who are married or cohabiting, and all women with dependent children or other relatives in fact have two major work roles; a paid and an unpaid one (Sharpe 1984, Pollert 1981, Cavendish 1982, Westwood 1984). But as Hunt (1980) and time-budget studies and other studies of housework (Wyatt 1985, Maynard 1985) have shown, employed women are slightly more likely to get help with their housework from men than are non-employed women, although as a consequence employed women end up with a very long working day (Walker and Woods, 1976) compared to men and to women who are not in paid employment. Hunt's (1980) research also suggests that women without children, but married or co-habiting, may get substantially more help from their partners towards housework than they do once they have children, especially if the latter group cease paid work at that juncture. The previous level of help also does not seem to be restored if there is a subsequent return to employment later. As one husband said to his wife in Hunt's study, when she complained about his unwillingness to take on household tasks or responsibilities in recognition of the fact that they both had paid jobs; 'I didn't ask you to work. If you can't cope in the house chuck the job in'. (Hunt, 1980, p. 109) Nevertheless, despite the unwillingness of men to assist with the unpaid work of running a home, the evidence seems to suggest that such 'help' (the very term indicates an assumption that it is an extra or a favour rather than a duty) is more forthcoming where a woman is in paid employment. Both the Milton Keynes and the Sheffield studies indicate this quite strongly, although there appear to be very few households where tasks and responsibilities are shared equally.

The opportunities for leisure for employed women are not only bound up with time available, but also with the perception of time and the legitimacy of leisure, which I shall turn to shortly. The other major disadvantages attached to paid employment which may affect leisure are the nature of the job done, pay received, the particular hours which are worked (especially if these are unsocial hours, which not only includes night work and weekends, but also 'twilight' working, common in jobs like cleaning and part-time factory work and often chosen because it allows husbands with day jobs to look after children whilst their partners are at work) and the physical and mental toll taken by the requirements of the job itself. Chambers (1985) in a study of shift work for the Sports Council found that shift-work was a greater constraint on women than on men in terms of preventing the women from doing the leisure activities they wanted – there was too little time and they made fewer friends or were unable to see the friends they did have. Unsocial work hours also appear to increase the amount of home-based rather than community leisure that is available to women working such hours. The Department of Employment study of women workers (Martin and Roberts 1984) found that relatively few women work overtime compared to men, whatever their normal hours, although as the study also points out, there is almost no evidence to tell us why this is so ('choice', no opportunities etc.) But overtime does not seem to be a significant constraint on women's leisure.

As I have already noted, women's employment is mainly within a narrow band of occupations and there is no doubt that some of this work is extremely tiring. Although clerical work, a major employer of women, is less physically demanding than factory work, cleaning or catering, it is also increasingly involving office technology, especially VDUs and computerization in general which may have undesirable and energy sapping effects on its workers, as well as reducing autonomy (Crompton, Jones and Reid (1982) West 1982). Factory work, as Cavendish (1982) and Pollert (1981) show in their ethnographic studies, is both monotonous and tiring and does affect the use of leisure time. Cavendish found that learning new jobs on the assembly line where she worked was particularly demanding;

> I was completely exhausted. I had terrible pains in my neck and back, and found it hard to keep up with the speed of the line . . . Most days I was worked so hard that I couldn't look up at all (p. 19)

although as familiarity with what was involved developed, so boredom set in and ways had to be found to divide the day up as 'Sometimes 7.30 to 9.10 seemed like several days in itself' (p. 113) and 'You wanted to make sure to use the breaks for yourself' rather than for getting further ahead with work or redoing something previously done badly or wrongly. (Cavendish, 1982, p. 112). Cavendish found that for married women with children any spare time outside their job, childcare and housework was spent in relaxation at home although single women did manage to go to pubs and dancing. Pollert's (1981) study of tobacco workers found that many of the women in such work looked older than they were, 'skin pale, tired and drawn' (p. 112) and their 'time off' often consisted almost entirely of housework. Even holidays often got used for this too; as one woman said, 'I think you need a rest now and then, apart from your holidays. Because when you're working and you've a holiday, you sort of leave everything, your odd jobs that are piling up' (Pollert, 1981, p. 119). This led to 'getting on the club' (i.e. taking sick leave) either to have a rest or catch up on housework.

Martin and Roberts' (1984) research on women in employment suggested that stress levels were higher amongst women in factory, unskilled manual, semi-skilled domestic work and sales workers. Dislike of a job was also a significant factor in causing high stress levels too. Stress caused by a job is likely to affect both other unpaid work *and* leisure. Women in non-manual jobs in the study were also far more likely to say that they enjoyed their work and had other than instrumental reasons for being employed. This is bound to affect other aspects of their lives. In the Milton Keynes research I found that women in higher paid secretarial jobs, administrative jobs and the caring professions not only were more likely to have a high proportion of out-of-home leisure but were also likely to say that they had developed new leisure activities as a result of who they met at work and the facilities offered;

> Before I came to work here (Large parts warehouse for major car company) I did very little out of the house. Now I've joined (the company's) badminton and squash clubs and met lots of new people. (married woman, two children, administrative job, Study A).

The Rapoports studies (1976) of dual-career households also suggest that where women are in well paid non-manual jobs with a high level of intrinsic interest in the job itself, a greater level of leisure activity in and out of the home is likely. Although the kind of job done is obviously very important there are also other advantages attached to women simply being in employment which crucially affect their leisure. One of these is having their own money and not having to justify its expenditure to male partners (this gives both financial and emotional bargaining power in the household), something which emerges from almost all the research on married women in employment and which is also important to single parents. Single women who have no children and have never lived with a male partner are less likely to see having their own money as an advantage but nevertheless in the interviews I did with single women, having disposable income was seen as a job plus which balanced out the amount of time it removed from possible leisure use. Women with jobs generally also have more status as individuals in their own right. Another advantage attached to employment which involves working with other women (which covers many areas of female employment) is the sense of shared sociability and friendship which this affords, both enabling breaks at work to be enjoyable and providing the possibility of after work shared leisure too. Sharpe's (1984) study of the lives of working mothers demonstrates the extent to which women who have been at home increase their confidence and improve their self-image by getting a job. A woman with a three year old child and a part-time job in a butchers' shop said to Sharpe;

> Before I worked I found it hard to talk to people, like I wouldn't be able to sit here and talk to you. I just couldn't make conversation with anybody. Since I worked here and meeting a lot of people I find that I can talk to people much better (Sharpe, 1984, p. 82)

Such confidence not only improves self image and status but as Sharpe says, enables women to become more self-assertive over a number of aspects of their lives, including their male partners, household finances and their leisure time.

Employment, even in low paid jobs with little or no intrinsically interesting content (evening cleaning, for example or waitressing) does then seem to provide both social and financial advantages to women in their pursuit of leisure. For married and co-habiting women being employed also seems to increase the chances that they will see themselves as having a legitimate right to leisure. A woman in the hosiery factory studied by Westwood who was organizing a day trip to Blackpool discouraged women from going accompanied by their husbands (although this had the effect of deterring some of the Asian women who saw the trip as not respectable) by saying;

> We don't want the men around. Christ, I see my husband every bloody day I don't need to see him in Blackpool, as well. We want a day out on our own for a change, get away from the kids and the house, not have them hanging around and findin' out what we're up to, up there. (Westwood, 1984, p. 92)

Westwood's study also emphasizes how important social events and rituals are in the workplace itself, whether it is birthday or marriage celebrations or eating food in the works canteen which wouldn't be available at home (for example some Asian women ate meat there but were vegetarians at home because of their husbands and families). Social events do of course also take place amongst groups of women who are not employed, but as Wimbush's (1985) research suggests, sometimes they are based on casual forms of paid work like party selling. Sharpe (1984) and my own research suggest that employed women are more likely than women outside paid work to be able to negotiate spaces for themselves for leisure, maybe because they have had to negotiate in a similar way in order to be in the labour market at all;

> Saturday night's mine. It's been a battle, getting it together in the end, because I find if I don't get time to myself I get very irritable and very resentful, as though everybody owns me, some bit of me, and there's none of me, that sort of feeling . . . I really enjoy Saturdays, I really look forward to them. I feel as though I can sort of shed me skin. (Marilyn in Sharpe 1984, p. 79, with a job, husband and two children)

What jobs seem able to do is to enable women to compartmentalize their lives, if not to the same extent as employed men then certainly better than women without paid employment. In the Milton Keynes research, employed women had more leisure interests and were better at protecting their leisure time from invasion by other household members than women without jobs;

> I just tell him I'm going out Wednesdays – if he don't like it it's just

too bad – I get tired and worn out from my job just like him, it's no different, you have to have some time your own' (shopworker, three children under twelve, husband railway worker Study A).

That compartmentalization is a good thing might sound rather antithetical to all those leisure studies experts arguing that different aspects of our lives ought to blend together, but compartmentalization does seem to be closely bound up with the development of attitudes which assert a right to leisure. This is especially important to most women whose unpaid work consists of fragmented tasks and responsibilities which are never-ending and often ill-defined. Employment provides the day with structure and routine, and as Coyle (1984) notes, women with jobs become used to organizing their housework, and childcare, round that routine. The loss of a job therefore, may present problems not only in relation to the loss of income, status, bargaining power, friends and enjoyment, but also removes routine, structure and the possibility of 'spaces' away from husbands and children.

3. Unemployment – no job, more play?

Until very recently, as Marshall has pointed out (1984) there have been many studies of the effects upon men of unemployment but none of women. But in the mid-eighties a number of studies have begun to appear which do address this issue (e.g. Coyle 1984, Martin and Wallace 1984). That the topic remained previously unexamined is as Dex (1985) argues, partly a consequence of the prevalence of the 'gender model' of explanation of women's employment (referred to at the beginning of this chapter) so that women, who were not 'expected' to work, were asked why they did, whilst men who were 'expected' to work, were asked why they did not. There was also an implicit assumption that if women did lose their jobs then they had a role waiting for them at home, which would render their unemployment much less traumatic than that of men who lost their jobs. As Dex says, studies of unemployed women have encouraged a greater emphasis upon the *meaning* of unemployment. Those studies so far completed have offered a rather complex analysis; 'unemployment as previously defined may not be a wholly appropriate concept for describing all women's experiences, . . . some women clearly have similar experiences of unemployment to men, and . . . some women have different experiences of unemployment from men' (Dex, 1985, p. 52). So for example in Wood's (1982) study of female redundancy, women were not found to receive their redundancy passively, nor was it the case that they thought of themselves as having less right to be employed than men, *but* their response to redundancy was more varied than would be found in a study of men, and some for instance decided to have babies rather than search for another job. Studies of male unemployment have found that women partners may also remain outside employment because it affects benefit entitlement for the household as a whole (Land 1981, Fagin and Little, 1984) rather than necessarily because no jobs are available to them, or because women think they should not be breadwinners. Stamp's small scale research (1985) suggests that the notion of a breadwinning wife may be more acceptable in households where both partners have gone through further/higher education.

I have already alluded earlier to the problem of deciding when women should be considered unemployed, because this definition does not follow automatically for women with no regular full-time employment. The studies on female unemployment have mainly avoided this problem by concentrating on women who have recently been made redundant. It is more difficult in a context like that of Milton Keynes, where women have given up jobs on moving to the city, usually following husbands or partners, and have been unable to find similar or other suitable work in their new location. Martin and Roberts (1984) noted that some women rejected the label 'unemployed' because they associated it with 'having nothing to do'; this was also the case in Cragg and Dawson's (1984) study.

For women who are what Martin and Wallace (1984) term 'committed to market employment' the loss of a job in circumstances they have not chosen (whether redundancy, ill health, or an enforced move to a different part of the country) is problematic in a number of ways. There is income loss, status and confidence levels may decline, friends may be seen more infrequently and former leisure activities may no longer be possible. Also, Martin and Wallace contend, the idea that unemployed women can just return to their roles as housewives and mothers is not applicable to women whose children have left home or who have no children or other adult dependants; they do assume other women can so return. Nor is the role of housewife particularly attractive to some women; Martin and Wallace found many who felt isolated but who did not feel that they lacked a role. The Martin and Wallace study is almost the only British research based on a large national sample of women made redundant from a cross section of regions and types of employment (although because they used large employment units, their research did not reflect the largest sectors of female employment, which tend to involve small units of employment.) Because of the timing of the research those in the sample who had not found alternative employment were still mainly using up their redundancy money, so the loss of financial autonomy had not yet become apparent to the same extent as it would later. Martin and Wallace note that the women involved had established before their redundancies a pattern of life which they expected to continue until they reached retirement age. What those women experienced was a considerable disruption to the routines they had grown accustomed to and a sharp decline in the number of people whom they met each day (e.g. from workplaces with over 100 employees to just the few inhabitants of their homes). 'The contrast between the directed activity and companionship of the work-place and the freedom, comparative isolation, and quiet of home and neighbourhood was sharp.' (Martin and Wallace, 1984, p. 233). The most frequently chosen activities which women took up or did more of to replace their jobs were housework, visiting, entertaining and going out with friends and relatives, gardening, knitting, sewing and other crafts and home decorating. In other words those things which as the previous chapter showed are the most likely choices of at-home leisure by women in a variety of circumstances.

These activities however were in Martin and Wallace's research sometimes closely related to the circumstances and skills of women who had recently been made redundant. So knitting and sewing were mentioned most often by former garment workers who used their previous work skills to make clothes for their families and friends.

Women with the most privatized domestic lives went out most to see friends or relatives. Only a minority of women (35 per cent) had taken up new activities on becoming unemployed, and the likelihood of having done so was found to decrease with the length of time spent out of work. Despite filling up their days with household tasks and responsibilities previously done after their employment was over for the day or week, 30 per cent of the sample said that they had time on their hands every day. Most of the women in the study were too young to retire and few had young children, or saw pregnancy as one way of using this extra time. Loss of friendship is another aspect of unemployment which may affect women. Although Martin and Wallace found that only one-fifth of their sample said most of their personal friends came from work, most had enjoyed being with work-mates and nearly all women had some personal friends from work. As Martin and Wallace note, the importance of work friends too is that they are easily accessible, whilst other social networks require a higher degree of organization of contacts. Hence it is not surprising that most women reported a deterioration in social life since becoming unemployed. Symptoms of stress were also common, ranging from one-third who reported stress as a direct result of losing their jobs to nearly half the sample who said that they had experienced periods of depression. Asked whether they preferred (paid) working, two thirds of the women replied in the affirmative and the researchers report that those who had been unemployed longest showed no more signs of reconciliation to their situation than those who had more recently become unemployed. The main message of the Martin and Wallace study then is that redundancy does have a dramatic effect on the *quality* of women's lives.

Coyle's (1984) study of women made redundant from clothing firms in Yorkshire during 1981/2 is based on a much smaller sample than Martin and Wallace's research. Coyle suggests that explanations of women's 'acceptance' of redundancy which are based on their femininity or assumed domestic role are insufficient; 'women's responses to redundancy have to be understood in the total context of work, family *and men*; men as managers, trade unionists, shop floor workers and husbands' (Coyle, 1984, p. 34) Some husbands were pleased their wives were losing their jobs as it meant they could do more work at home – 'He likes me at home because he always had to do the dinners, now everything's done for him . . . He was pleased. But I miss my bit of money' (Coyle, 1984, p. 42). The loss of jobs did not simply mean less money and more housework (both of which in themselves have important implications for leisure) but also loss of social contact; 'I don't think I've really got over it yet, because you're missing something' (Coyle, p. 52). More serious even than these aspects of unemployment for some women was the loss of routine 'I was very settled at Roger Firth, you get up in the morning, you go to work, you come home, you know what's going to happen, you get into a sort of routine . . . I didn't like being without a job because I've always had a job' (Susan Peters, Coyle, p. 68). Similar views about loss of routine were also apparent in the Martin and Wallace study 'I feel as though I'm drifting – it's only when I'm working with people that I feel as though I have a purpose to life or a pattern to life. I can't come to terms with the life I lead, doing housework over and over' (machinist, Martin and Wallace 1984, p. 256). Other women in Coyle's study talked of loss of confidence in themselves, extreme boredom and time 'dragging'. One woman who had found another job said it was not only the money which pleased her 'Now I'm working, I'm enjoying my freedom' (Anne McKenzie, p. 87) as a single parent, which when she had been without a job seemed more like a trap. Some women did come to like being at home but even they spoke of devising routines for their housework, in an effort to create some kind of time structures for themselves which previously had been provided by their job. Also the home when unemployed, no longer provides the kind of base it might for leisure;

> I don't go out. I miss the money and I miss the work. It took me out of the house and I wouldn't need to use any gas or electricity. I don't put anything on at the moment but if it gets any colder I will have to (Coyle, 1984, p. 105).

A cold quiet house with little to do but housework is no substitute for a job, nor is it conducive to leisure, which involves an attitude of mind as well as activities and enjoyment. The previous pace of work, even though it may, combined with housework and childcare, have been exhausting, is also missed, because many women have got used to compartmentalizing their lives so there are spaces for everything – when there is too much time to spare neither the compartmentalization nor the routines work so well;

> I'd rather be rushed off my feet. When I was working I used to come home, dash to the shops, a quick flip round the shops, come home start the tea, flash round with the hoover and duster. I'd dash up and have a bath and be off somewhere for the evening. Now I just seem to be missing out on everything . . . your life's come to a standstill (Coyle, 1984, p. 113).

I found amongst those women in the Milton Keynes study who defined themselves as unemployed (36 out of 168 in sample B) that the experiences were very similar to those reported by Coyle and Martin and Wallace, regardless of the women's home situation, responsibilities and household size (although it was clear that those with young children tended not to define themselves as unemployed even where they had recently lost a job or were intending to look for a job). Those women, on the other hand, who described themselves as full-time housewives or mothers, were much less likely to think of themselves as isolated (even though some of them apparently were) and rarely, except for women over 65, thought that they had 'time on their hands'. However this latter group of women did seem to be making an effort to develop household and childcare routines (although often with great difficulty because of the number of contingencies which cropped up every day) which enabled them to have some time and space for themselves each day of the week. There were major differences to be found between the employed, unemployed and those who had no job, but who did not define themselves as being unemployed. The first group saw themselves as having a legitimate right to leisure, and on the whole were able to organize themselves and their lives so that they got some leisure on a fairly regular and predictable basis. They had a mix of friends from their paid work and elsewhere, were relatively self-confident and had some, even if limited, financial independence; they also had the most out-of-home activities of any group. The unemployed found it difficult to develop a household routine, had few friends that they saw on a regular basis, did not see themselves as having the same right to leisure as when they had been employed, felt socially isolated, lacked confidence and frequently got depressed, had given up more leisure activities than other women and went out less often; they also (where married or co-habiting) felt and were dependent on their partners financially (single parents living on benefit felt the loss of a job as acutely but still retained control over their meagre finances) and felt very constrained by having to ask if they could have money for bingo or bus fares or a magazine. Both the unemployed group and the 'non-employed' group had more home-based and domestically linked leisure time and interests than the employed group of women. The 'non-employed' group seemed less socially isolated than the unemployed group, although they also lacked confidence, and were unable to set aside predictable time periods for their own enjoyment; they were more able so they said, to ask for money for their own use. They also tended to draw their friends from other women without jobs, whereas the employed and non-employed tended to have a mixture of friends with and without jobs. The non-employed also got least help with their housework from other household members, although unemployed women also reported that their husbands were much more reluctant to help with housework than they had been when they were still employed.

It is also evident that male employment and unemployment influence female leisure and although a detailed examination of this is not possible because of limited space, it is useful to explore this briefly.

4. Male employment and women's leisure

It is not difficult to predict the kinds of effects which male employment is likely to have on female leisure. The effects range from the disruption of housework caused by unsocial hours of work or shift working to the incorporation of women into their husband's or partner's work where there is a need or expectation that various tasks will be undertaken by women (phone answering, typing, book-keeping, entertaining, visiting clients or customers etc.). Both Finch (1983b) and Edgell (1982) note that certain types of professional work are likely to absorb large amounts of men's time and are likely to reduce the amount of time women who live with such men have to themselves. But this is also true of other kinds of jobs, including manual ones and self-employment, especially if low wages or other considerations mean that a considerable amount of overtime is also worked (Hunt, 1980) or where hours are irregular or involve long time periods away from home. Men's ability to compartmentalize their own lives obviously does vary with the kind of occupation they are in, but to the extent that this is possible, it is likely to reduce the extent to which women are able to do the same, especially if they are not themselves in employment.

My research found few married or co-habiting women whose partners were in employment whose free time did not suffer from the demands made by the timing and nature of their partner's work. This ranged from having to cook two evening meals (one for children, one for a partner who came in much later) to having to wash workclothes at frequent intervals. Only one quarter of the 135 women with partners in sample B said that a partner's job never affected their relaxation and non-work activities, although it is significant that in sample A, partners' jobs were thought to affect leisure very little. This is only partly accounted for by differences in lifecycle and personal circumstance, so it may be that some women are more able to over-come such constraints than others. The Sheffield study by Green, Hebron and Woodward (1985b) found that employment of partners was not particularly significant as something which 'cropped up' to stop women having time to themselves, and only 4 per cent mentioned problems to do with husbands or partners as a reason for doing leisure activities less often than they would like. It is possible that the question of male employment and its effects on female leisure will emerge more strongly in the in-depth interview stage of this project (not yet available at the time of writing) because it was something which I found was much more likely to be raised in detail in an unstructured individual or group interview than in response to a questionnaire. The Leeds study (Dixey and Talbot 1982) did find that male work patterns and work roles were a significant factor which affected women's leisure especially for women not in paid employment;

> Daily life for housewives in Armley revolves around the routine of the breadwinner . . . the work patterns of men are accommodated . . . 'Most days he's out (to work) at half past seven at the latest and God knows when he'll be back. You never know when to expect him' . . . The husband's work role sometimes caused conflicts of interest, whether it was because work was brought home . . . or because the husband needed to switch off to recuperate . . . either way the wife was excluded (Dixey and Talbot, 1982 p 27).

Male employment then does have a marked effect on the leisure of some married or co-habiting women, although much also obviously depends on the nature of the relationship women have with their male partners, the kind of job men have and its hours, and women's ability to assert their own needs over that of their partners. My own evidence suggests, although this cannot be used as a basis for wide generalizations, that employed women are more able to overcome or ignore the constraints potentially placed on their own leisure by male employment.

5. Male unemployment and female leisure

As I indicated earlier, much of the research carried out on unemployment has focused on male unemployment rather than female unemployment, but recently this balance has been somewhat redressed. The relationship between unemployment and leisure has become as popular a topic in the 1980s as in the 1930s which is closely related to prevailing ideologies and economic conditions in our society (Deem, 1985). The debates around the 'informal economy' have drawn attention to the difficulties the unemployed face in being involved with the informal economy because of their lack of financial resources (Finnegan 1985 and Pahl, R. 1985). This is something likely to affect both men and their female partners, although R. Pahl's evidence from the Isle of Sheppey study seems to indicate that women may lose more leisure time as well as activities, because of the greater demands placed on them in relation to housework and the exigencies of making ends meet on a much reduced budget. Research on male unemployment suggests that after the initial stages of relief at not having a job, depression, boredom and laziness may develop, to be replaced if unemployment becomes long term, by some more permanent adjustment to a life without paid work (Hill 1978). These stages are likely to be traumatic and disruptive for women too, especially those who are also without paid work, but who are used to being in control of the household during their partner's previous working hours, not only for their housework but also for their free time and leisure activities. Finance is likely to be a real problem, especially since as Land (1981) and Bell and McKee (1984) note, women whose husbands or partners are unemployed are less likely to engage in paid employment themselves because of the loss of benefits likely to ensue from this. The Sheffield study (Green, Hebron and Woodward 1985b) found that one group of women particularly constrained in their leisure were women with unemployed partners and that the constraints related not only to money, but to disruption of household routines and tasks and the difficulties of taking leisure time when male supervision is close at hand over housework. There has been much debate and controversy about whether male unemployment increases the extent to which men participate in housework, and the available evidence, whilst demonstrating that housework participation does often increase if men are unemployed, also suggests it is frequently done with bad grace (Chappell 1982, Marsden 1981). Hayes and Nuttman (1981) also argue that the early stages of male unemployment are seen as temporary by those involved and this too may increase the amount of housework done at first, with a falling-off later if short-term unemployment becomes long-term unemployment. Fagin and Little (1984) found that for some families in their study, male unemployment had a quite profound effect on the quality as well as the standard of living, easily spilling over into leisure and affecting all members of the household. My Milton Keynes research suggested that the female partners of unemployed men, particularly where the women were also unemployed, had the least leisure time and least leisure interests of almost all the women studied. Compared to unemployed women with employed partners for example, unemployed women with unemployed partners, whilst suffering in the same way as other unemployed women with the difficulties of compartmentalizing their time, also found that general feelings of depression and debilitation affected both what leisure activities they did and their ability to perceive spare time as leisure time.

Clark (1984) in an analysis of post-redundancy male shift-workers noted that stage of life cycle is an important factor in the response of households to unemployment. Where male unemployment coincided with a transition from one stage of the life cycle to another, radical changes such as a move to other parts of the country (or emigration) were contemplated if redundancy had also severely affected the friendships and social networks of the household. Bell and McKee (1984) reported in their study of couples in Kidderminster that whilst male patterns of leisure spending were often continued, albeit at a reduced level, during male unemployment, women often had no access to personal spending money. Further they found that wives' lives were likely to become increasingly privatized as a result of male job loss, either because friends withdrew or because men exercised social control over their wives' social lives. 'The impression is also given in a few cases that husbands *control use of domestic space*, visitors come only with *his* approval even if they are *her friends*' (Bell and McKee, 1984, p. 21). Male unemployment does then appear to have a variety of effects, almost all of them detrimental, on female leisure and these appear in the main to be different effects from those occasioned by female unemployment. Once again they relate to mechanisms of power and control which men exercise over women.

6. Employment and unemployment; the impact on leisure

I have tried in this chapter to explore some of the interconnections between employment or its absence and women's leisure. It has been suggested that in order to do this satisfactorily, it is necessary to take into account a range of factors, of which gender is only one. So the type of employment, life cycle stage, ethnicity, hours of employment, household composition and power relationships between male and female partners may all be significant influences on how employment and unemployment influence women's leisure time, leisure activities, the perception of a right to leisure and the ability to compartmentalize work of all kinds and separate it out from leisure. What does seem to emerge is that female employment may be as important in structuring women's experience of leisure as male employment is in organizing and determining men's leisure. Women in employment frequently, although not always, have greater control and autonomy over their own lives and hence greater control over their leisure, than women who are not in employment despite the existence of patriarchal forms of workplace control too. Thus the notion that the most enviable lifestyle is one in which leisure and work flow into one another without perceptible boundaries is dispelled and there is certainly little evidence to suggest that the unemployed, whether women or men, produce in their households a quality of life which supports an experience of leisure which is in any way superior to that enjoyed by those who remain in employment.

CHAPTER SEVEN

Leisure and life cycles

In the previous chapter the main focus was on the relationship between paid employment, unemployment, non-employment and forms of leisure. It was suggested that paid employment is particularly important for women's leisure, not only because of the independent income which it may provide, but also because it offers a structure within which leisure is both possible as a separate category and is seen as a legitimate right. But employment status is not the only major influence on women's leisure; others include education level, access to transport, children, men and male power relations, household composition, ethnicity and class. Women's leisure is however, not necessarily always influenced by the same factors throughout adult life; while some like ethnicity remain constant, other influences increase, diminish or appear/disappear at different stages. Life events like the birth of children, marriage and divorce, illness, the necessity to care for dependants and the process of ageing itself are all extremely significant in shaping leisure. It is sometimes assumed that the norm in leisure, particularly in fields like sport, is to take up an interest or activity and continue it until old age or injury intervenes; those who do not follow this pattern are seen to be deviant. In fact, as previous chapters have suggested, for women at least, the reverse of this may be true – most women do change quite radically over their adult lives in terms of which leisure interests they have, when these take place and with whom. Some of these changes are forced on women, others are chosen; some are the product or part of wider social changes (for example the decline in cinema attendance and the shift to home videos). Others reflect the economics of commercial leisure provision (more stately homes and parks to visit, bicycles aimed specifically at women) whilst further changes mark new ideas about health and well-being (the current medical lobby for more exercise) or simply fashion and style changes (if jogging suits are fashionable or dance clothing, they may encourage their purchasers to try the activity too).

1. Conceptualizing the Life Cycle

Some of the first attempts at conceptualizing this process of change in individuals' leisure over their lifetimes were made by researchers looking at family leisure. For example the Rapoports used the term 'life cycle' to describe this method of analysis in their book *Leisure and the Family Life Cycle* (1975). The Rapoports were particularly interested in how life cycle changes would affect the use of leisure resources and the implications of this for policy-making on leisure. They devised a theoretical framework which utilized a number of key stages which covered people's lives, ranging from young adulthood (roughly 16/19 to 26/29) through the 'establishment phase' (roughly 25 to 55) to the 'later years phase' from 55/60 years onward. Within each of these three main phases the Rapoports conceptualized a series of sub-stages, so that, for instance, the 'establishment' phase is seen to consist of an early period in which people acquire families, occupational interests and other commitments, a middle period in which children are growing up and the family are settled in a particular area, with family-centred leisure activities, and a late phase when children have left home.

Inevitably because the concern in developing this framework was the family, there is in the Rapoports' work a focus on married couples and on what are considered 'normal' ages at which certain things should be accomplished. There is however also an assumption that life is likely to continue on an upward curve from young adulthood through to retirement, so that the mid-establishment phase for example is one in which personal spending and consumption patterns are seen to be high and to include things like foreign holidays and the purchase of leisure equipment. Leisure then is at least partly equated with expenditure on consumer leisure goods or services. Perhaps in the 1970s assumptions such as these were more soundly based than now, especially for middle class families, but in the 1980s whilst people may still hold such aspirations, the realities of job loss and unemployment for school leavers and older adults are as the last chapter pointed out, very close at hand. Also problematic are the assumptions made by the Rapoports about the harmonious relationships likely to exist between couples in relation to leisure. Power differentials and struggles are hardly seen to enter into the process, whether between women and men or between adults and children, even though subsequent work by the same researchers has suggested that leisure is shared very unequally between couples even when both are in professional employment (Rapoport and Rapoport 1976, 1978). In fact it may be the case that the kinds of struggles in which women engage over their lives and leisure do relate to the events of their life cycle, just as divorce rates tend to peak in the early years of marriage and then again after twenty years of marriage, but this assumption about struggle as part of life events is not part of the Rapoports' framework.

Using the notion of the life cycle then, is not without its problems, particularly in relation to the assumptions about 'normal' patterns of behaviour and the times when this behaviour is likely to occur in people's lives. The correlation between age and life events will and does vary however. Demographic data for example suggests that working class women are likely to marry and to have children at younger ages than their middle class contemporaries. Women who remain single and childless are likely to have a very different pattern of life to those who marry or co-habit, but divorce and/or single parenthood can also drastically affect a pattern which might otherwise continue in the sorts of ways the Rapoport framework suggests.

But despite all the drawbacks to using a life cycle approach, there are also important advantages so far as the study of women's leisure is concerned. Dixey and Talbot (1982) in their study of Armley used different ages as a way of organizing diaries of weekly evening activities. There are a number of distinct patterns which emerge from that analysis, which are particularly significant for the exploration of which women are interested in bingo, with single young women showing no interest, but older married women turning to bingo in their thirties and forties, and pensioner women also showing a considerable interest in bingo. The life cycle concept is also helpful in correcting the tendency to see women and leisure as being all about young married women in their twenties and thirties with small children, something which is very easy to do as this group seem to symbolize many of the difficulties and constraints which make leisure difficult to achieve. This group *is* a significant one for all sorts of reasons, but it is important to see it in some kind of perspective which also takes into account the other experiences of women's adult lives, and which can encompass the notion that leisure is not static either in content or meaning, but shifts over time. What is done at twenty may be discarded reluctantly at twenty five and taken up agian at fifty; something enjoyed by a young mother may have no appeal at all to a single teenager or a woman whose children have themselves become adults. As long as the concept of life cycle is not used to bracket away other considerations and social divisions (ethnicity, class, employment, status, for example) then it does have a place in the analysis of women's leisure. For the remainder of this chapter I am going to focus on the conjunction (which is, as noted above, subject to some variation) of life events and age as a way of looking at how both the nature of leisure and the constraints on it alter over the life of individual women. There is also scope here for future research which tries to reconstruct personal leisure biographies (although as a method this has disadvantages related to the unreliability of personal memories) and/or uses longitudinal data, perhaps from studies constructed originally for other purposes.

2. Young women and leisure – adolescence, courtship, (un)employment

There is an obvious problem here with what or rather who, counts as young women. If we take the Rapoports' (1975) age range, then it goes from about sixteen through to the early twenties for some women, less for others. I have assumed here that it covers only teenage girls.

One of the essential features of this phase is the emphasis on being single and childless, and alterations to this status take place at different times for different social groups. Indeed Talbot and Dixey (1982) suggest a qualitative difference exists between teenagers and women in their twenties. For adolescents leisure is likely to be perceived very differently from the way it is for older people; the difference between teenagers with and without a job is also an acute division, as a study by Wallace (1985) on the Isle of Sheppey underlines. Much relevant work is actually on adolescent girls who have not yet left school, and most of it is on working class girls too, although there have been one or two attempts to redress this balance (Lees 1985). The leisure time preoccupations of teenage girls tend to focus around relationships with boys, clothes, records and tapes and activities like dancing (McRobbie 1978; McRobbie and McCabe 1981; McRobbie and Nava, 1984) although much of the research has not taken into account variations based on membership of ethnic minority groups. Femininity is seen as an important part of teenage female culture, but so too is an ambivalence about sexuality and a considerable degree of sexual oppression by males (Scraton 1985, Cowie and Lees 1981) aimed at controlling girls' own sexual behaviour. Friendships with other girls seem important to teenage girls' leisure only until they develop relationships with boys, at which point same-sex friendships begin to disintegrate (Griffin 1985b, Leonard 1980). Clearly this latter development may take place at different times for various social groups and may differ for members of ethnic minority groups and girls who are not heterosexual. Male dominance over women's leisure can be seen to commence very early – whilst girls are still at school the attitudes of males towards their behaviour, dress and where they go can have a significant effect on the leisure activities and leisure locations chosen by girls, hence the popularity of girls' toilets at school as a gathering place for friends to talk (McCabe 1981). Once girls leave school male constraints on their leisure are likely to continue, whether these operate at an individual level, particularly for girls with boyfriends, or at a more generalized level, in terms of problems about where it is 'safe' to go and when, because of fears of sexual harrassment or assault. Griffin (1985) found in her study of working class girls in Birmingham that the most common leisure activity was 'dossing', that is 'hanging around in a group of "all girls together"' (Griffin, p. 63) either in their immediate neighbourhood or at weekends by going into the city centre. Willis (1985) has also drawn attention to the extent to which young people are to be found hanging around shopping centres, and the contradictions between the intentions of those shopping centres to entice in consumers and their attraction also of young people whose lack of spending power means they are often seen as a nuisance and asked to move on. Griffin (1985) found that the pub was a major source of entertainment, even though for under 18s this was illegal, because places intended for the young usually required an entrance fee. Those still living at home also found that their parents tried to stop them, often unsuccessfully, from going to places where boys and alcohol were to be found. Youth clubs on the whole were not very popular, since they were, unless a girls' only night was organized, usually dominated by boys, who commandeered all the facilities and were also liable to be noisy and physically aggressive, both to girls and to each other. Black girls faced not only sexual but also racial harassment, both of which were major constraints on their leisure time. Girls without friends living near to them found that it was difficult to become involved in out-of-home leisure; this was particularly the case for unemployed girls who tended to become absorbed into domestic labour and as a result of this, and their lack of money, they often became socially isolated. Girls in employment had more money and social contacts and if they had no regular boyfriend might make arrangements to go out in a group;

> We've known each other for years and we decided once we left school we don't want to split up. So we've kept in touch, there's a group of us. We go out together, or sit in here listening to records and drinking. We go to this private social club, it's local, they all know us. it's good (Griffin, 1985, p. 192).

The leisure of young women may be relatively unvaried; it will certainly, except for a very few, contain little or no sport (Scraton 1985, 1986), it will involve relatively few locations, and is likely to revolve around the home and immediate neighbourhood. Middle class girls may be able to venture further afield and have more varied interests (including certain kinds of sports) but face similar problems about male and parental control over what they can or cannot do. A small study of 16+ school leavers in Milton Keynes by Brown (1985) found that many more women than men had a regular partner and that where this was the case social life tended to revolve around that partner. Brown found few males or females had hobbies; most spent time at home or at the home of friends on things like TV, video, music, games and talking. Only those women who had become mothers went out infrequently; others went out two or three nights, mostly to pubs or nightclubs. The only sports women did in any numbers were swimming, walking and pop-mobility or keep-fit. Commercial leisure provision in the city was felt to be poor for young people, and what was provided was either inaccessible by public transport or too expensive. Leisure centres and youth clubs were not much used.

Leonard's (1980) study of young engaged couples in a Welsh town also suggests that for the women leisure was unvaried, and that there was a tendency for young women to lose touch with their female friends once they were 'courting' seriously, something which was not replicated for their male partners who continued to see their male peers. Leonard found that pubs, clubs and licensed dance halls were popular with Swansea residents in their late teens, but that whilst males would go to these locations either alone or in company, females would usually go with either a female friend or, and more likely, with a boyfriend. Most of the young people studied by Leonard were still living with their parents, and she uses the concept of 'spoiling' to explain the way in which those parents serviced their offspring with domestic services, money and emotional support, which has implications not only for the leisure that this makes possible for young women but also for the constraints it may place on mothers in relation to their own leisure. It was also found that girls spent much more time with their families than did boys, although the latter may spend more time at home once they are engaged and trying to save money. Leonard's fieldwork was actually carried out in the late 1960s so that although she argues that things have not changed much since then in Swansea, elsewhere in the British Isles there have probably been more changes, two of which, rising unemployment amongst young people and a greater likelihood of couples living together prior to or instead of marriage, are likely to have altered young women's leisure. Unemployment drastically reduces the amount of money available for leisure, leading to the kind of isolation talked about by Griffin (1985) and increasing the likelihood that pregnancy and/or marriage will become part of their social reality, although Griffin warns against seeing marriage simply as an alternative to employment. Co-habitation is likely to affect female leisure more than male leisure; in the Milton Keynes study I found that of women under twenty-one, those who were living with men were least likely of their age group to be involved in activities outside the home with anyone other than female relatives or their male partner. Furthermore living together does not necessarily mean that the division of labour in the household is any more equitable than in the homes of married couples, and it appears to have similar consequences to marriage for the male supervision and approval of women's out-of-home leisure activities.

Talbot and Dixey (1982) found in their study of Armley that 'the recreation of teenage girls . . . revolved around the 'big three' of drink, boys and discussion. The latter was usually about adults, themselves, boys, jobs, sex' (Dixey and Talbot, 1982, p. 41) and this broadly fits with the picture other researchers have found for young women in their late teens who are single.

Overall then, women in their late teens do seem largely to be divided in their leisure choices according to whether they are employed and whether they have a regular partner. Whilst going out is something widely associated with teenage girls, especially to discos, dances and pubs, much of this declines if a regular boyfriend is acquired or if unemployment reduces the money available for leisure. Whilst at-home activities of this age group, on the whole, reflect generational as well as gender considerations, the greater tendency for women rather than men to spend time at home and the importance of talk or discussion (to call it gossip is to belittle it) are two of the more enduring features which are likely to continue on into the next phases of the life cycle. For those women who are mothers in their late teens, this later phase is already reached.

3. The twenties and thirties – marriage and cohabitation, childbearing and rearing

The first important point to make about this group is that the correspondence between age and significant life events is far from perfect. So, as Dixey and Talbot (1982) note in their study of Armley, this age bracket encompasses considerable variety in employment and household situation, and in whether or not there are young dependent children. There is an enormous difference between the young, single, employed, women living alone or with friends and the married woman with no paid job and three under fives. Compare for example the profiles of Ms B and Mrs C in Chapter Two; one is extremely active in out-of-home leisure, the other spends virtually all her leisure time in the house, with Ms B doing virtually no housework (remember Delphy's (1984) view that work you do in the house to maintain yourself is not really housework) and Mrs C doing a great deal. Whereas Ms B has few constraints on her leisure other than those common to all women (for example restrictions on travel and in access to public spaces), Mrs C is constrained by her husband who is very absorbed by his own leisure and who won't stay in and look after the children in the evenings so she can go out. She is also restricted by her total lack of independent spending money, by her sole responsibility for the house and children and by the absence of local friends as well as by transport difficulties. But not all women in that situation – no job, children, husband – are necessarily constrained as much as Mrs C. The more middle-class Mrs A, despite having a three year old child, and only part-time (and hardly lucrative) work selling books, nevertheless has a much more lively social life and more leisure interests outside the home. Mrs A also has a more supportive husband who is prepared to undertake his share of household tasks, including childcare, particularly if she wants to go out in the evening, either for leisure or for work.

Variations on the basis of social class and marital status apart however, the majority of women in this age group in the Milton Keynes study spent most of their leisure time in rather than out of the home, kept there principally by childcare, housework, lack of money and very often by their husband's leisure and/or job. Evening classes, clubs and sport were all activities done frequently by single and childless women in their twenties and thirties, but done very infrequently by women who were mothers and by women who were married. The former group were also the most likely to spend precious leisure time with their children (recognized as both a pleasure and as a tie by most women to whom this applied in my random sample). Shared activities with partners were mainly confined to watching TV or home videos, relaxing at home, having friends or relatives round for meals and occasional visits to pubs or restaurants. In-home leisure was often linked to domestic chores – baking, sewing, knitting. Single parents sometimes had more freedom in the sense of not having to negotiate power struggles with a partner, but with young children and little money they too, in this age group, had little out-of-home leisure which didn't involve children. Asked about activities given up, all except single childless women mentioned dancing, going out with female friends to pubs, restaurants and night clubs, and many kinds of sport, from team games like hockey to badminton, fell walking and tennis. Not all women missed these activities;

I always felt when I was younger that it was great but a bit hectic – I was literally out every night except Sunday, and I never helped my mum in the house; I just ate meals and slept there. I had a lot of money then, and it all went on enjoying myself – I miss that bit but I prefer my life now – I like to sit down in the evening with a book and some chocolates – to all that dashing about. (woman in early thirties, with two children aged three and seven, husband a quality control inspector)

Others did miss their previous life and the freedom they had had;

I used to love going out dancing on a Friday night with all my mates from work – I used to spend the whole week preparing, buying and trying on clothes and make-up, thinking who I'd meet, what I'd say, what I'd drink – I felt I could do what I liked, when I liked – I really do miss dancing, but . . . (husband) would never let me go, he'd be worried I might meet someone else and the kids misbehave if he has them in the evening (twenty eight year old part-time cleaner, eighteen month old baby and three year old, husband a warehouseman)

Another woman who had won prizes for disco dancing as a teenager said sadly 'My husband says I'm too old for dancing – but he just doesn't want me to go'.

Dixey and Talbot (1982) found that women in their twenties, whether single or not, and whether mothers or not, all placed high emphasis on 'socialising', either in the house or out of it, with friends and husbands or boyfriends. The twenties group also went out more often than any other group except teenagers. The researchers found that on the whole married women with under fives and childless women went out about as frequently as each other – two or three nights per week, but women with school-age children went out much less often (on only 20 per cent of the evenings in the sample week as opposed to 57 per cent for childless wives and 53 per cent for those with young children). Women in their twenties were also found to be ambivalent about their adolescence – it was seen by over half the sample as both the most enjoyable and least enjoyable period in their lives. On the other hand Dixey and Talbot thought that they discerned the decisive age watershed for leisure as being the thirties, who spent fewer nights out of the house than any other group and had nearly two-thirds of them feeling dissatisfied with this state of affairs. Housework occupied a good deal of time for both the employed and the unemployed, much of it associated with school-age children. Favourite ways of spending an evening were "reading quietly", "relaxing when possible", "with a good book and some chocolate", "drink at home listening to music" (Dixey and Talbot, 1982, p 43). The differences between the Dixey and Talbot findings and the Milton Keynes study illustrate one of the difficulties inherent in using the life cycle approach – that is, the overlap between age and life events is not always well matched. So that whereas in Milton

Keynes there are a lot of women in their twenties and thirties with school age or younger children, this may be less the case in more established urban areas, where there is a greater mix of household situations amongst women in their twenties, but perhaps greater homogeneity amongst women in their thirties. Nevertheless, looking at the group who do appear most constrained – mothers of dependent children who also have male partners, it is clear that most of them fall into the twenties and thirties age bracket. In the Milton Keynes sample B they were the most dissatisfied with their lot so far as leisure was concerned, and the group for whom least is provided. They have little money (where they are in employment much of their wage packet goes on providing basic necessities for their children and husbands), they need childcare for over and under fives, in the day and evenings or at weekends, and they are at the stage in their lives where their partners, if employed, are least likely to assist with the housework (Hunt 1980) and when their housework is at its peak (Graham 1984). Their past leisure pursuits and interests are likely either to be outgrown, too expensive, too time-consuming or not permitted by their partners. They are, if without employment, the most socially isolated group and they are least likely to have access to good transport (for example a car) during most of the week. The Sheffield study (Green, Hebron and Woodward 1985a and 1985b) also found that mothers of dependent children went out significantly less than other groups of women.

The extent to which the same findings emerge over several studies concerning the stage of life cycle, if not the exact same age groups, suggests that the periods when women have small children, under or over school age, are the most constraining so far as out-of-home leisure and in-house undisturbed leisure are concerned. *But* we also need to recognize, in working out any kind of leisure provision for this group, or in exploring what kinds of changes in structures and ideologies are necessary to alter this situation, that this stage does not represent the life-situation of *all* women. The classic nuclear family of two adults, non-employed wife and two dependent children is not the commonest form of household in the UK; in 1982 the average household size was 2.64 persons, with only 27 per cent of households consisting of more than three people, but 56 per cent of one or two persons, including children; and it does not last for ever. It is however probably an important stage for so-called 'family leisure', (Rapoport and Rapoport, 1975) resulting in all those visits to stately homes, leisure centres and parks, fairs, seaside resorts and so on which according to *Social Trends* 1985 are continuing to increase. But to call something 'family leisure' gives it a cosy feel, whereas in fact much of that leisure may be conflict-ridden and beset by struggles between men, women and children over where to go, when, how and who cuts the sandwiches/drives the car or escapes to the nearest pub when it all gets too much. No prizes for guessing who usually wins these struggles.

4. The forties and fifties

The distinguishing feature of this group is not so much their age, as the fact that they are unlikely to have young children, and indeed in some cases children will actually have left home by this point. It is also a period during which some women will undergo a divorce, leaving them not so much single parents as in the previous group, but single women living alone. Still other women (but a minority) will never have married at all. Many women of these ages will be in employment and are significantly more likely to be in employment than women over 24 and under 35 (Martins and Roberts 1984). Hence they are likely to have at least some independent money to spend and are also able to make use of the time-compartmentalization afforded by being in a job. Women in their forties and fifties are likely, unless disability, ill-health or care of elderly dependents prevents them, to be involved in a considerable amount of out-of-home leisure. It is this group which sustains many of the organizations and clubs which as Chapter Three showed, comprise a sizeable proportion of women's leisure; they are also a mainstay of evening classes and bingo clubs. The Rapoports (1975) suggest that women at this stage may be more involved in couple-leisure. But the Milton Keynes evidence suggests this is subject to class variation and also depends on the kind of relationship women have with their partners. Also crucial are the division of labour within a particular household and whether males are heavily involved in separated leisure.

For couples whose children have grown up, the division of labour in the household does not necessarily become more equitable even if the tasks lessen and both are in employment (Hunt 1980 and Edgell 1982). Indeed it is only likely to be more shared, even then often reluctantly, if men become unemployed. Also couple-leisure is not necessarily egalitarian in the forms it takes; as a group of women from a branch of the Business and Professional Women's Club said in my research about their own and couple leisure;

> quite a lot of us are active in other groups too . . . the Operatic Society, PTAs . . . the Mentally Handicapped Group, Women's Institute . . . most of us are in full time employment too . . . but even though we have more time now than when our children were young, women's leisure occurs less often than men's . . . is looking

after a pet or cooking a meal for your husband's business colleagues
leisure? (Deem, 1982)

Shared leisure with a partner may mean going somewhere you don't
want to go or with people you don't like; it can also involve bringing
into the home friends of your partner whom you might exclude if
you had the choice, something divorced women are often pleased to
have got away from. (Pahl, J, 1985a and Wimbush 1985). Not all
women in this age group necessarily have children who have left
home either. Whilst those 'children' are likely to be teenagers and
hence in many cases not interested in so-called family leisure, they
may nonetheless expect to be 'spoiled' by their mothers (Leonard,
1980). Also unless they are old enough to drive a car or own a
motorcycle, then their leisure activities may involve their parents in a
good deal of fetching and carrying no less wearing (and often at
more unsocial hours too) than the escorting of younger children to
their leisure activities. Edgell (1982) found that for some 'mid-career'
families in his sample of professional couples, the absorption in
employment (mostly by males) and domestic work (mostly by
females) meant that they failed to take advantage of expanding
income and a decline in household workload brought about by no
longer having young children. However, once they had moved into
what Edgell calls the 'late career' stage, there was usually 'an increase
in leisure time available to husbands and wives, especially the latter'
(Edgell, 1982, p. 81).

Whilst this group of women are highly involved in out-of-home
leisure, both with their partners and with other women, they are also
likely to be involved in in-home leisure too, with a greater focus on
crafts, music and creative pursuits rather than the 'sit down and relax'
or TV watching leisure engaged in by younger women. In the Milton
Keynes research (Study A) I found this forties-fifties group to have
the largest number of in-home leisure activities of any group. Out of
the home they are not merely noticeable for their involvement in
organized leisure, but also for the leadership roles which many of
them, and not just the middle class ones either, take in clubs and
organizations. Sometimes this was explicitly seen as a substitute for a
job; this *was* invariably by middle class women.

(Why did you get involved in the WI committee?) My children were
growing up and I found myself with time on my hands; my
husband's one of those old-fashioned types who don't like their
wives to work, so I decided I'd get more involved in the WI – I've
also recently become a parish councillor but without the WI I'd
never have had the confidence – I've learnt an enormous amount
from being in the WI – it really isn't just jam and cake making. I've
done photography, calligraphy, local history and how to run a

meeting and speak in public. (woman in late forties, three teenage children, husband civil servant Milton Keynes Study A)

Whilst sport is not a major pre-occupation for this group in the conventional sense, yoga, keep-fit, walking and rambling are popular with the more active women and amongst those who fear they have 'gone to seed' whilst their children were young. Friendships with other women are also very important, and with fewer of the constraints previously in existence (children, house-work, money) it is probably easier to sustain such friendships. Friendships are very important for out-of-home leisure; in the Milton Keynes study I found that women who had no close friend living nearby were much less likely to be engaged in out-of-home leisure, for a variety of reasons including shyness, lack of confidence, fear of travelling alone on public transport and absence of motivation.

The Dixey and Talbot (1982) study suggests that those women in their forties are in 'the best period of leisure' (1982, p. 43), whilst those in their fifties may perhaps be 'unsure of their leisure roles' (1982, p. 43) as perhaps for some ill-health (sometimes associated with the menopause) and other signs of approaching old age (including possible retirement from employment) appear. In Armley whilst the fifties group still went to bingo, other activities very popular with the forties group (eating out, going to pubs and cinemas) became less important although women's groups based on the church were especially important for certain women (and indeed were dominated by women of this age). Nevertheless this period between forty and sixty does seem to be one in which leisure, often for the first time since the early twenties, once more plays an important role for women. Yet the needs and interests of this group are often forgotten both by policy makers and by commercial providers, despite Fetherstone and Hepworth's (1981) argument that for both sexes the later years of middle age are a major focus of consumerism. There is a suspicion here (or more than a suspicion) that gender stereotyping sees ageing women as having little sexual or personal appeal, whilst men of a similar age (equally groundlessly) are seen as having sexual attraction and personal charm and hence only the latter are a major target group for consumption of all kinds. Demographic trends in Britain show older men who divorce and remarry are likely to choose younger women; older women are less likely to remarry at all and if they do so tend to marry men of the same age or older (*Social Trends* 1985: Annual Abstract of Statistics 1984); It is possible that women who do not want to live with men again after divorce have learnt that life is more enjoyable without men around of course!

5. The Sixties, Seventies and beyond

It is often at this point in their lives that women begin to reap the consequences of a lifetime of playing subordinate roles. Low-paid employment, part-time jobs with no pension entitlement, motherhood of declining significance except vicariously through grandchildren, men dying earlier than women, lack of experience in being independent and fending for themselves, poor health; all contribute to a situation in which many women of over sixty have few resources (both financial and otherwise) with which to enjoy themselves. Yet the picture so far as leisure is concerned is enormously varied; whilst some women, particularly those still in their sixties, are very active, in a variety of clubs and organizations, bingo, evening and day classes and in-home interests, others are very socially isolated, have little money, are in poor health and have few interests of any kind, and ironically have far too much 'leisure time', which they are totally unable to fill. Once women are sixty they are eligible for OAP activities. Although some women hate the image that these often have 'They're for really old people; the only time I went to anything like that they all kept mistaking me for the helper' (woman in Milton Keynes, aged seventy one) others are appreciative of what they offer. Other things available to OAPs which are much appreciated for the potential leisure activities they offer include cheap bus travel and rail travel at concessionary rates on a rail card, although here it is often couples who travel and many women are apprehensive of travelling even short distances on public transport alone. The ways in which male control over women's sexuality and right to be in public places operates is such that it continues to be a major constraint for most women all their lives; also older women are often frail and feel more vulnerable than younger fitter women.

In the Milton Keynes study I found that in Study B many of the questionnaire refusals came from women over sixty 'I don't have any leisure now dear . . . so I won't waste your time filling it in'; or 'I think you must mean younger women'. But in the 'women-out-of-the-home' phase I found some incredibly active women in their sixties and seventies (see for example Mrs D in Chapter Two) who put younger women to shame, just as I have often been impressed on polling days during local elections by very elderly ladies who are still sufficiently politically committed that they insist on making their way to the polling station unaided, when many half their age 'can't be bothered' to walk half a mile to do the same. I interviewed once a group of women ranging in age from fifty to seventy who had for many years been members of a tennis club. None of them any longer played tennis, but the club and its social activities remained a major focus of their leisure, and they also had as a consequence an impressive grasp of the history of the club and the community where it was located. The Sports Council and other organizations have found that the revival of tea dances in the afternoons in town centre halls or leisure centres are extremely popular with women in their sixties or over, who had perhaps thought their dancing days gone for ever, but to whom dancing was once again able to assume importance in their lives. Dixey and Talbot also found this in their Leeds study.

There is then considerable variation at this point in the life cycle, and physical and mental health play a big role in this. Those women who are in poor health may find it impossible to go out (Dixey and Talbot 1982 found that the over seventies were much less likely to go out than those in the sixties age group) and may find their leisure increasingly consisting of radio and TV. Only visits to and from relatives and friends, if any are still around or in contact, occasionally break the monotony. The social isolation of old women is not the only factor that makes their lives more difficult. The loss of many of their social roles may mean that they are not only lonely but also feel their lives lack purpose, although if they still have a partner, housework is likely to continue to be done only by women. As one said to Dixey 'Well yes, you've had your life . . . well you can't expect to . . .' (Dixey and Talbot, 1982, p. 45)

Further, as Duquemin (1982) has noted in her study of a small number of women over seventy in a Devon town, not all old women have actually been wives or mothers, nor do they necessarily have families around them, and so some may reach seventy with a very different view (and perceived very differently by others too) of themselves, their femininity, status and social life. Women who have been single all their lives are likely by the time they reach seventy to be well used to being independent and doing what they please, whereas a recent widow may find it difficult to adjust after a lifetime of housework and dependence on a man, and is less likely to be self-sufficient. Jerrome (1983) in a study of women in their fifties and sixties who are unattached and lonely and who seek companionship through friendship clubs, points out that in fact a group of lonely women may actually be counterproductive, because they lack the social skills necessary to make new friends. She found that the kind of friendship women expected to find through clubs was also important, being usually based on previous experiences. Women who expected to find an 'exclusive' friendship in which they and their friend went everywhere together were often disappointed, whilst those who saw friendship as being a balance between inputs and rewards, rather than exclusivity or 'taking more than giving', were more likely to find new friends.

The later years of life for women then may initially be quite full of activity, both inside and outside the home, but circumstances can change rapidly, and ill-health, loss of a partner and friends through death, and trying to live on a meagre pension can mean most leisure is spent at home and is seen as coping with boredom rather than a satisfying way to use leisure time. The 'time on my hands' syndrome found amongst unemployed women (Martin and Wallace 1984) once again surfaces for many women, and leisure, far from being a scarce resource, may come to be dreaded. Of women over sixty in both the Milton Keynes studies but especially Study B, very few had access to a car. Dixey and Talbot (1982) found that 96 per cent of women over seventy in Armley did not have a car in their households. Many women of these ages have never learnt to drive and even if they are living with a partner who can, cost or ill-health may cause a car to be given up anyway. Public transport and walking are often dreaded for fear of being attacked or just ridiculed, particularly by adolescents standing on street corners. So ageing brings in its wake restricted leisure and perhaps an over-abundance of 'spare time'.

The life cycle and leisure

This chapter has, I think, shown both the strengths and weaknesses of the 'life cycle' approach. It *is* important to get a picture of how women's leisure changes over their lifetime in response not only to age, but also life events and phases, from adolescence through child-bearing and marriage to children leaving home and retirement from paid work and becoming an old-age pensioner. It is certainly not the case that women spend all their post-teenage years wishing they were young again and could do the same leisure activities that they did then. Furthermore, while it is the case that some activities disappear, never to re-emerge, others do re-appear and, like dancing, may be enjoyed as much or more than previously. The life cycle approach also allows us to see how much the constraints on women's leisure are shifting ones and the extent to which some constraints are part of the power, ideology and social structures of patriarchal relations between men and women at all ages. Thus struggles between women and men over childcare may lessen or disappear in late middle age, but struggles over housework may continue. Women whose children are grown up may regain some of their former freedom for out-of-house or at-home leisure, but are still subject to collective male social control over their freedom to go about in public places without fear of sexual harassment and attack. Women who have returned to employment are likely to have some independent income (as well as benefiting from time-compart-mentalization) to spend on leisure but the continuing gap between female wages and male wages and women's inferior position in the labour market (Garnsey, Rubery and Wilkinson, 1985) continue to mean that women's disposable income is almost always less than a man's and that their equal right to leisure is not accepted fully by a male dominated society.

The disadvantages of the life cycle approach can really be summarized in two ways. Firstly, age and life events cohere differently for different social class and ethnic groups and also there are often regional differences. So it is always necessary to over-generalize in order to make the point and there are always women to whom, for example, childbearing occurs much later or much earlier than the 'norm', or who do not have children at all. Nevertheless, as Delphy (1984) points out, the existence of marriage as a relationship of unequal power between women and men affects and influences the lives of all women whether they marry or not, because marriage is so much part of the structure and ideological assumptions of industrial societies. The expectation that women will have children and the ideological baggage and structural implications of this for the way society is organized also affects all women whether they have children or not. But the implications of marriage and children for leisure may well be different for those who experience only one or neither. The second disadvantage of the life cycle approach is that it is difficult to incorporate other significant life events which are not necessarily age linked. For example, unemployment and divorce are both extremely consequential for women's leisure, but whilst some age-linked patterns are discernible in these two phenomena, their occurrence cannot be predicted very accurately in age terms. However, despite these drawbacks, the life cycle approach is, as I said at the beginning of this chapter, a useful corrective to the tendency to see women's leisure and its associated constraints as being mainly about women in their twenties and thirties with young children. It also enables us to trace different activities across different stages of women's lives and discern which constraints on leisure are temporary and which are more enduring.

CHAPTER EIGHT

Towards more play and less work

In the last seven chapters I have attempted to sketch out some of the dimensions of women's leisure, provided a detailed case study of Milton Keynes, examined some of the key contexts in which leisure occurs, considered women's roles in sport and explored the interconnections between employment and leisure, as well as discussing the relationship between life cycles and leisure. Such analyses have not only told us what we know but also pointed to the gaps in our knowledge about women's leisure – there are still many questions which remain unanswered. It has become evident, if it were not before, that leisure is a phenomenon which is not easily separable from other aspects of women's daily lives and which is closely interwoven into everyday routines. It has also become clear that whilst women do experience certain constraints and problems in relation to enjoying leisure or having time and space for it, there are also enormous variations in the leisure activities and modes of recreation and relaxation available to women. Gender is a powerful structuring and ideological force, but it is certainly not the only factor which shapes women's leisure. Although given the neglect and ignorance of women by much previous leisure research, it has been necessary to make the case for taking gender fully into acount forcibly. But at the same time this does not mean that other crucial factors like race and class should be omitted. Nor, as I pointed out in Chapter 6, should we necessarily throw out *all* the research findings of gender-blind social scientists and sports scientists about leisure, for example the job-leisure link. Employment can be one powerful lever for getting not only time but also the legitimate right to leisure. It is, furthermore, important to see *leisure* as the problem rather than women (Stanley 1980) and to seek the explanation and resolution of constraints on women's leisure in the power relations, institutions and ideologies of capitalism and patriarchy, as well as looking at leisure facilities and provision themselves. There will always be some women for whom securing adequate leisure presents no difficulties, and a few for whom life seems to provide rather too much 'time on their hands', but there are a large number who fall somewhere between these extremes.

1. The question of definition

The definition of the concept of leisure is something which seems to have bedevilled all leisure researchers. The notion of leisure as something different and separable from paid work is very much a legacy of male working class experience in the period since industrialization commenced. An early contribution by feminists to the study of leisure was to point out that this particular conceptualiza-tiion actually fails to come to terms with either the work or leisure experiences of women who are not in paid employment (McIntosh 1981, Griffin 1981). The term leisure has little meaning to some women, as several researchers have found out, although that does not necessarily mean that their lives are devoid of all enjoyment and relaxation. The conventional notion of leisure as particular kinds of activities taking place in clearly demarcated places and spaces and seen as an escape from, an extension of or recuperation from a job is, in any case, applicable to less and less people now, with the continued existence of mass unemployment, early and other forms of retirement and growth of part-time employment. But leisure's reputation has continued to grow and develop in new ways. Some commentators (Jenkins and Sherman 1979, 1981) have begun to discuss the ways in which leisure may be able to replace work. Such discussions are usually, but not always, based on the premise that if technological developments put people out of jobs, they may also permit society more leisure time and facilities if managed in the right way. Leisure has also been seen by various bodies and government as a substitute rather than a better alternative (à la Jenkins and Sherman) for paid work, which can be used to control the young unemployed (Carrington and Leaman 1983); sport has been a major part of this 'work-substitute' strategy. Women have usually only entered these debates on the periphery; for reasons discussed in Chapters 4 and 6 women are often not counted as unemployed (even if they are) nor seen as part of the 'dangerous classes' who need to be controlled lest they rise up and riot (except if they are outside an American nuclear base). But women have not escaped the 'rediscovery of leisure' since they are seen as a 'target group' to whom the message about sport and leisure must be spread.

The structural reasons why women don't participate in leisure and sport are however largely ignored in favour of a 'give them crèches and let them play sport' attitude which sees difficulties residing in individual rather than social and economic determinations, just as offering leisure pursuits to the young unemployed often fails to take a wider view of why the young in that situation are dissatisfied and alienated. But although such approaches are to be deplored for their narrow views, the net effect of these strategies and related debates has been to widen out definitions of leisure and blur the boundaries between work and leisure. At the same time feminist analyses of housework and research by economists, sociologists and anthropologists on the 'informal economy' have brought to our attention the existence and importance of work which is not organized and renumerated in the public world of the formal economy and labour market. (Pahl R. 1985, Maynard 1985, Finnegan 1985). Some of this work has drawn attention to the difficulties of demarcating what is unpaid work and what is leisure; for instance is tiling the bathroom unpaid work or leisure; is jam-making for sale at a W.I. market stall more akin to work than making it for home consumption or to give to a friend? Now it may be the case sometimes that it does not matter either to the individual concerned or to anyone else. But it should be evident from the exploration of women's lives in this book that it *does* often matter, both to those individual women who are aware that there is little space in their lives for relaxation and leisure and to those of us who are committed to improving the social position of women. Having a life style in which leisure and work spill over into each other with neither being distinguishable from the other is fine for those who choose it, but it is more than apparent that many women have extremely limited choices and might well prefer a life in which it would be possible to clearly separate at least some part of their time and energy and reserve it for leisure, relaxation and recreation. Hence the suggestion made in Chapter 6 that women with jobs are more able to structure and organize their routines, in such a way that there are clear spaces for leisure and a perception of a *right* to leisure, is something which is extremely important in developing ideas and visions about what women's lives could look like. And such visions are, as Eisenstein (1984) points out, an extremely important part of feminism's commitment to changing women's present subordinate position in society;

> In my understanding of the term 'feminist' then, I see an element of visionary, futurist thought. This encompasses a concept of social transformation that, as part of the eventual liberation of women, will change all human relationships for the better (Eisenstein, 1984, p. xiv).

In essence then, whilst not pretending to have solved the question of how leisure is defined (although it must be related not only to time and space, enjoyment, pleasure and relaxation but also to the quality of those phenomena) it does seem to me now although at one time it did not, that it is important to hold on to the concept of leisure. Further it should be seen as something at least analytically and hopefully sometimes in practice too, separable from forms of work and other life obligations (even though work and obligations may feed in to which leisure, what and where). If we argue that the concept of leisure is totally inapplicable to women, then there are no grounds for arguing that women should have a legitimate right to it, as many men already perceive themselves having. Clearly holding on to a vaguely defined concept cannot be more than a starting point, just as saying that people have a right to decent housing does not necessarily solve the problem of what kind of housing or where. But it is an important starting point to asking firstly what do women want from leisure and secondly how are they to achieve this.

2. What do women want?

This sub-heading is deliberately taken from an article with the same title by Rowbotham (1985) in which she raises issues about how women should attempt to change the world. Following Eisenstein (1984), she sees the options of competing with men on male terms or else withdrawing into a female retreat as dead ends for most women, which leaves the difficult question 'How do you create and assert an alternative in a world that is not your own? How can such an alternative prevail or become a defining element for transformation?' (Rowbotham, 1985, p. 49). What Rowbotham then does is to examine some of the ways that other subordinate groups in the past have tried to counter the dominant culture, whilst coming to terms with the ambivalence of both resistance to and acceptance of that dominant culture. Feminist values, Rowbotham suggests, however oppositional, are part of the existing culture. Women's oppression involves not only social differences and inequalities, but also biological difference. So for example, in relation to sport, men do not have to worry about the impact of pregnancy upon their performance in the sports field nor whether continuing to do sport during pregnancy will affect an unborn child but both of these are cultural as well as biological and sometimes difficult to disentangle. The women in sport issue, as we saw in Chapter 4, has had to cope with the question of whether there are biological or cultural reasons to explain why until recently men have outperformed women in many competitive sports (Dyer 1982) and it is only when these are disentangled that any theoretical and empirical progress is made. Women's identities are also affected by trying to transform existing relations between women and men, and so it is not only men but women too who are 'desperate to hang on to certain valued differences' (Rowbotham 1985, p. 53). These kinds of struggles and contradictions are very evident in the study of women's leisure. Many women who are aware that they do not have access to the same range of leisure possibilities, either inside or outside the home, as men, are also reluctant to do anything about this if it will disrupt, for example, their sexual and/or household relationships or what they may perceive as their control over what happens inside their homes (for example men sharing childcare or housework). So the woman who scrawls across a questionnaire 'I am quite happy being a housewife – I chose it and I like my husband' or the woman who refuses to be interviewed because it will upset her husband may well have contradictory views about her life, identity and personal relationships. Nor do women who are not heterosexual or who do not live with men escape the implications male cultural dominance has for their leisure, so that they too experience constraints and may have contradictory or inconsistent ideas about the gap between what leisure they have and what they would like to have and why the latter may not be desirable. Hence Rowbotham's view that 'a vital aspect of feminist politics asserts the value of women's existing social experiences as a means of gaining space for women to determine what they want to hang on to in particular historical circumstances' (p. 54) is an important one, as is also her emphasis on the need to transform male culture. So, for example, there is little possibility of changing women's leisure experiences whilst men still believe that Saturdays are for watching sport or going to the pub because those two beliefs and the activities they involve are themselves part of the reason why for women Saturdays are often not about leisure. But equally women's leisure is not going to be transformed overnight by them taking up competitive sport or going to lean on bar counters consuming gallons of fizzy beer (although there will be those who will want to do these things or already do them). Change might develop from an attempt to learn from situations (whether in the peace movement or in new forms of 'negotiated' adult education) where women use co-operative rather than hierarchical forms of organizing and doing things, or where they combine leisure with helping others.

I know that my emphasis on the importance to women's leisure of women being engaged in some form of paid employment will be seen by some as a negative or backward step, but what it does is to build on the experience of those women who already exercise more control over their lives than do some of their unwaged sisters. This isn't tantamount to saying that life is just about struggles in the labour market or that what happens in economic production is more important than what happens in the household nor that many aspects of women's employment are not oppressive. We can also learn a lot from the ways in which some women organize their household lives and gain enjoyment from non-commercialized forms of leisure, including aspects of their unpaid work and domestic obligations, whilst recognizing that some aspects of this are exploitative and need to be changed.

There is also a crucial issue here about how change is to be achieved within the existing culture and sets of power relationships as well as through more radical transformations of the conditions of social existence. Reform and change are often counterposed to each other as though reform were really not worth the effort because it does seek to alter things within the existing framework, whereas change is conceived of as something much more radical and hence inherently worthwhile and worth waiting for, even though the scale and nature of what are being sought are such that there is little or no possibility of them being achieved in the foreseeable future. I am certainly not opposed to visions of radical social transformations, indeed they are much needed, but unless such changes are to be brought about by widescale violence and the use of force, there does need to be a measure of consent to those changes taking place. In societies such as the UK, it seems more likely, given its history and present state of development, that there will be consent for change through reform rather than revolution. I shall shortly be looking at what kinds of changes are necessary for the improvement of women's leisure. But before I do that there is another aspect of 'what do women want' which needs exploring.

This is related to cultural diversity amongst women. It has I hope been clear throughout the book that whilst women experience some constraints and experiences in common there are also many differences between them, whether these are to do with class, ethnicity, marital status, sexual orientation, employment, domestic obligations or life cycle stage. Much of the research now going on into women's leisure takes many of these factors into consideration. But ethnicity has by and large been absent. This is not to say that no-one has ever taken into account the leisure experiences of women from ethnic minority groups (there were Afro-Caribbean and Asian women in my own studies for example) but that the dimension of ethnicity and the importance of coming to terms with racism in understanding the lives and leisure of black women has tended to be left out. As Barrett and McIntosh (1985) have pointed out, this is because much feminism has tended to be white feminism and has focused on the experiences of white women, without considering how black women's lives are affected by not only class and gender but also by racism. There is a need for feminist theory and feminism to rethink many of its categories and ideas which it has used in the past and which may display white racism in the way that Barrett and McIntosh suggest.

However the issue is as Barrett and McIntosh recognize, rather more complex than this. White feminists have as they show, resorted to myths and stereotypes about, for example, Asian women (that they are passive and submissive and always restricted by arranged marriages, for instance) or have ignored the importance of race so that the experiences of a group of black women workers, for instance, are seen as no different from the experiences of white women workers, (although this is not universally the case amongst such research, see Westwood 1984). But there are two other complicating factors here. One is that as Barrett and McIntosh say, care has to be taken not to lapse into complete relativism, where no criticism at all is advanced of forms of gender oppression which exist in the cultures of other ethnic groups. So, for example, although the family forms of Afro-Carribbean women may tend in some respects to give them greater control over their leisure than white women living in nuclear families; this does not mean that Afro-Carribean women do not experience constraints on their leisure, some of which are related to their gender as well as to racism. The other complicating factor is to do with the practicalities of carrying out research. For example in one particular area of Milton Keynes there is a Bangladeshi community which appears to suffer from all manner of social disadvantage and whose experiences tell us quite a lot about Milton Keynes as a city and community, particularly about the extent of racism and tolerance of cultural diversity. But since none of the women in the Bangladeshi community speak sufficient English either to have completed a questionnaire or been involved in an interview, their experiences do not form part of my study. Of course in a larger project funded by an external funding agency it would be possible to overcome some of these difficulties, by employing researchers with a knowledge of relevant languages or who are themselves members of the particular ethnic minority groups the community comprises. The evidence however suggests that even where this would have been possible it has not been taken on board. There is no excuse for this failure to take ethnicity and racism into account and it is something which future work in the field of women's leisure urgently needs to remedy.

3. Changing women's leisure

There are, as the preceding chapters have shown, a number of important factors which seem to differentiate those women whose leisure experiences, whilst still subject to certain constraints, are nevertheless both extensive and satisfying (to them) within the confines of what is socially and economically available. There are other women whose leisure experiences are limited and fragmented to such an extent that it might almost be said that they do not really have any significant leisure separable from the rest of their lives. But it is in this group which seem to form the majority, although there are undoubtedly those women (in particular very elderly women and those who have recently lost their jobs) for whom having too much leisure presents a problem. It is possible to discover from the experiences of women whose out-home and in-home leisure seem less constrained than many of their sisters, some of the reasons why the former are more successful than the majority in overcoming constraints on their leisure. Some of those reasons are cultural, some structural and others ideological. It would be easy to dismiss all of them as idiosyncratic and as the products of individual choice, but this would be to miss the point that choices are made within sets of social and economic circumstances over which people living at a particular historical conjuncture have little control.

Crucial factors separating women whose leisure seems least affected by constraints from those whose leisure seems very constrained, include having private transport (usually but not invariably a car), an independent source of money (even if the amounts involved are quite small), some form of employment, a fairly high degree of confidence in themselves and determination to do what they want, a sense of a legitimate right to leisure, and a network of support which may range from a friend or partner to a whole household or group of people. These things in themselves do not tell us anything about the kind of leisure that women may be engaged in nor where it takes place; it may be the kind of leisure stereotypically associated with women (knitting, sewing, the WI) or it may be that it includes activities like sport which are more usually associated with men. These six factors do not exhaust the possibilities, but others seem to have different effects on different women. So, for instance, single women do not invariably have leisure-filled lives; some middle-class women seem more constrained than some working-class women despite the former's undoubted economic and social advantages. There are women with children who negotiate round the problems of childcare, although women with adult dependents generally are not easily able to overcome the barriers to leisure that this kind of caring presents. Some women who live with men are able to establish their own leisure, others appear unable so to do. Then there are those women who perceive that they are disadvantaged in relation to leisure and those who do not necessarily see it in that way but who nevertheless are extremely constrained; both groups may have contradictory views about what if anything needs to be changed to improve their situation. And even those women who in leisure terms seem the most advantaged are still subject to overarching ideological and structural constraints which confront all women in pursuit of leisure; notions about the role of women and about what are appropriate activities for them and where they should or can go, low pay in women's jobs as compared to men's jobs, lack of childcare and education for the under fives and so on.

Seen in this context it is possible to group the kinds of changes which are required under three main headings – creating an environment in which women's leisure is safe and practicable; leisure provision, both commercial and public as well as individual; and changes to women's social position. The first two are certainly amenable to some changes or reforms within the existing system, whilst the last can certainly be improved within existing frameworks, although that will not necessarily achieve some of the more dramatic changes necessary.

4. Creating an environment for women's leisure

When people talk about changing leisure they usually mean changing what is provided, rather than the context in which it takes place. However, changing the provision without also changing the environment in which it occurs may do no more than redistribute the activities and interests of those women who already are less constrained in their leisure. There are in existence policies about leisure and sport in many local authorities (it is sometimes called 'recreation') but like other aspects of local government these tend to exist in isolation from other kinds of policies and departments which are in fact closely related. So transport policies, housing and education, all of which are very relevant to leisure, are either completely separate departments or within different tiers of local government. Yet for example, good reliable public transport and particularly forms of night transport which women would feel safe using, are a major part of making women's community leisure possible. Home-based leisure is very much influenced by the quality and lay-out of housing and the proximity of housing to leisure facilities is also of crucial importance. Street and footpath design and lighting can make an enormous difference to whether women feel safe outside the home in the day and after dark. Provision of childcare facilities for both under fives and school age children after school and in holidays can free mothers from at least some part of their obligations towards children so that they can enjoy their own leisure without spoiling their children's leisure. Education for girls could open up many more work and leisure possibilities than it does, especially in the area of physical education, and boys' education could include much more emphasis on domestic work and parenting. Funding of women's groups and organizations, even if these are not just leisure-oriented, can help build up the network of support that women need in order to enjoy and demand the right to leisure. Many of these things would be difficult to achieve at the time of writing because of the severe restraints on local authority spending (although some local authorities including the GLC, have managed to move in some of the right directions) but there is no evidence that in the past when spending restrictions were less of a problem that many policy-makers thought of leisure in this wider and more imaginative sense. Of course creating an environment which is structurally better adapted to women's leisure does not remove the ideological barriers which exist in either public or private places about where women 'should' go and what is appropriate activity for women. Women are also often deterred from leisure by forms of sexual harassment, violence and assault which emanate from men; but these forms of control of women and female sexuality are often condoned by both the ideological construction of masculinity and by ineffective public implementation of the law in cases of rape and violence against women, often occasioned by beliefs about the trivial nature of such offences.

Racial harassment of people using a leisure centre or bus is much less likely to be tolerated or unremarked upon than sexual harassment, which is often treated in a jokey rather than serious manner; both forms of harassment are liable to be treated as less important where women are the recipients. More effective implementation of existing legislation, including the Sex Discrimination and Domestic Violence Acts, would in itself help to alter the climate within which women's leisure takes place. Changing the environment for women's leisure is important not only because of its impact on men and the way in which patriarchal relations of power work, but also because it would actually encourage women not only to be able to use their leisure but also to see that they have a right to such leisure in and out of the home.

5. Leisure provision for women

The whole question of leisure provision is a difficult and complex one, but it is also an important one. Now of course it is the case that some forms of leisure do not need to be 'provided' in the sense of goods, services or facilities – relaxing, dozing, daydreaming, playing with children, walking – are all things which do not in the absolute sense need to be provided for. But most leisure does involve provision of some kind, whether it is indirectly through housing layout and pavements, or directly through tapes, videos, novels, the cinema or bingo. As Clarke and Critcher (1985) and others have indicated, much contemporary leisure and sport is heavily commercialized and infused with ideologies about consumerism, so that even activities and interests which appear to be very privatized, like reading a book or watching TV or drinking alcohol at home are actually heavily shaped by commercial interests. This is certainly true of many of the things which make up women's at-home leisure, whether it is reading 'Woman' magazine, or a 'Mills and Boon' novel, or knitting with 'Sirdar' wool, as well as applying to out-of-home leisure like bingo, visiting a wine bar or health club or going swimming at a leisure centre. But there is here a crucial difference between leisure provision for men and leisure provision for women, in that most of the decisions about provision for women are made by men. So not only does leisure provision reflect commercial and also 'public-provision' ideologies about the place and function of leisure in peoples' lives; it also reflects patriarchal ideologies about the roles of women, what it is appropriate for them to do and where it is appropriate for them to go, and the provision itself is frequently based on stereotyped notions of femininity. The stereotypes tend to classify women into either young sex-objects who need discotheques and wine bars, or mothers who require sewing classes and romantic novels. Women who want to take courses in electronics, learn to play football or take up mountain climbing, or who would like to go for a drink in an all-female environment without being harassed by drunken males, are in the main not catered for except by small groups of non-commercial 'alternative' providers.

Public provision might be thought to offer more possibilities than commercial provision because it has a greater chance of being influenced by changing views about women's social position; for instance there are many more women in positions of influence in local government than in private companies, some local authorities now have 'equal opportunity' policies, and national bodies like the Sports Council have specific policies on the importance of women as a client group. But much public provision, whether it is leisure centres with no crèche facility or photography evening classes open to all but with male tutors and male students interested only in 'glamour', is not necessarily better than commercial provision. This is partly because of the 'detached' view of leisure and recreation policies which many areas of local government and national bodies display – leisure is in one slot or budget head and safe transport in another. There may be ladies mornings at the leisure centre, with nice 'lady-like' sports available – swimming, badminton, table tennis but not a suitable bus to get there or, weight training, five-a-side or circuit training; or day time classes in flower arranging but expensive and miles from public transport. Who looks after children whilst women have leisure is left to Social Services, the Education Committee or more usually these days, to parents (which usually means mothers). Aerobics for unemployed women is a good idea but often advertises for customers by preying on the worries most women, but fewer men, have about their size, weight and shape. Women's keep-fit is usually entirely different to men's, and is about 'keeping in shape' or 'getting into shape' rather than about developing physical strength and power. There are also class barriers in public leisure provision as well as gender ones. I found in my research that many women are unable for financial and domestic reasons to commit themselves to activities on a long term basis involving payments in advance and attendance over a number of weeks; the few activities outside the home which permitted more flexible take-up were extremely popular, for example pop-mobility on a 'pay-as-you-go' basis. Raising this issue with the local education authority in connection with evening and day adult education produced a system whereby you can pay by Access card (but still in advance!).

Commercial provision presents other kinds of problems. There are a few commercial providers who have recognized the importance to them of their female customers and hence set out to discover if they are providing what is required, as in the 1982 Dixey and Talbot study of bingo which was commissioned by the National Association of Licensed Bingo and Social Clubs. There are many others who provide for women in a stereotyped way – romantic novels, magazines with cooking and household hints, pink jogging shoes (so practical!), cheap cameras which take cheap and frequently nasty pictures but which 'even a woman can use', pink alcoholic drinks or sickly mixtures 'for the ladies'. A few providers have recognized the importance of extending their market to more women – for example a major cycle manufacturer has produced an entire range of bikes whose advertising is geared to women (significantly to their sense of 'mood' and colour). But the kinds of bikes made are still 'women's frames', useful to ride when wearing a skirt, but harder work than a man's frame and with significant disadvantages for heavily laden tourists or returning shoppers (a man's frame is more stable) and often with poorer quality components than the male equivalents. Drinks companies produce concoctions aimed at women, but don't give nearly as much if any thought to where women are going to drink them – a crowded pub where the bar is surrounded by beer-swilling men is hardly conducive to a woman's enjoyment of a night out but no doubt the assumption is that she will get her drink bought by a man or consume it at home.

The lesson which needs to be learnt about provision of all kinds is that it is not sufficient to recognize women as a client group or as a 'target' for increasing participation. What is required is not women's leisure thought up and administered by men, but leisure provision which is motivated by what women want and happens under their control. Some leisure provision might remain broadly the same – some women do want to read romantic novels or ride a woman's bike in pink with matching accessories – but undoubtedly new forms of provision would appear, and the requirements of women for more flexible leisure provision and co-operative rather than hierarchical or competitive leisure and sport could be realized much more effectively. Women with a variety of different needs and interests could be catered for, rather than only those who conform to stereotypes of femininity. Women could be encouraged to take up activities hitherto mostly male-dominated (climbing, photography) in a context where they are not put off by male gate-keeping and technical mystique. Leisure-provision locations could include places women already use – health centres, shopping centres, for instance and could be provided in local areas as well as in city and town centres. Childcare provision could be made at weekends, evenings and in school holidays as well as for the under-fives in daytimes only (the latter is usually the only form available at the moment). Leisure could be made available in single sex groups where required; the need of women to be able to relax in single sex environments is as important as their need to have some autonomous forms of political organization, although neither of these need preclude other mixed forms. In a women-only group women may feel safer, less threatened and more able to be themselves rather than conforming to male expectations or being ridiculed if they don't. A lot of this may sound utopian in the present economic climate, but some of it is not about finding new forms of funding or finance, but rather about using existing resources differently, and about exercising political will in a different way, directing leisure provision towards women rather than offering most of it to men and letting women gather the crumbs from under the table.

6. Changing women's social position

The last two sections have addressed some of the possibilities for reforming women's experiences of leisure, largely within the constraints of the existing social, political and economic system. But a really fundamental change in women's leisure necessitates changing the relationships, structures and ideologies not only of capitalism (which as Critcher and Clarke 1985 have shown, has not served human leisure interests particularly well) but also of male dominance. Very many of the constraints women experience not just in relation to leisure but in the whole of their lives, are crucially connected with the way men live, work, act and think. Women have less money for leisure because even in paid employment their wages are much less than men's pay; women are still supposed to be fully or partially financially dependent on a man and this is often reflected in public policies (Social Security benefits, taxation) as well as in houshold budgeting. Women are supposed to be sexually passive, and their sexuality controlled by men. Women's employment is affected by their actual or supposed domestic and child-care responsibilities and so too is their leisure. Girls are prepared for their domestic role at school; boys almost never are (Arnot 1984). This perception of the sexual division of labour is both carried by men who ignore their domestic responsibilities and transmitted to new generations of males who think that being at home equals leisure. Women both make possible the superior pay and conditions of men's paid work (which is not to say that the latter are always satisfactory either, since under capitalism they are not) and enable men's leisure to take place by shouldering a heavy burden of domestic labour, childcare and others forms of 'caring'. That women often manage nevertheless to turn domestic labour and obligations into leisure is a tribute to women's fortitude; but it is no excuse for leaving things as they are because not all women complain.

But it is not simply, as this book has shown, that men prevent or constrain women's leisure through their failure to undertake 'familial work' (Delphy 1984) or through their strangle-hold over positions of power in commercial and public decision-making circles. It is also the case that male dominance extends by controlling both the acceptable images of women; sex object versus mother figure, ballet dancer but not football player; and to policing public and private places so that for some women neither home nor the community provide safe places for leisure. This is as much the case for those women whose own personal strategies for achieving leisure can overcome other obstacles such as poor facilities or fragmented time schedules. A woman who goes running or visits the cinema or a pub alone, but whose enjoyment of these activities is spoilt by sexual harassment, actual assault or a barrage of questioning by her male partner when she goes out is still constrained by male patriarchal social and sexual control, even though she may appear to be less constrained than a woman who is prevented by her own fears of harassment, her belief that she is overweight or her husband's paternalism from engaging in any out-of-home activities at all.

Similarly a woman who successfully negotiates and bargains her way out of the house (or gets her male partner out of the house with her children so she can have some time to herself) is still constrained by having to conduct those negotiations in order to obtain leisure which men take for granted, although not in the same way as a woman who is frightened to go out for her own sake (rather than shopping or fetching children) and scared to take time off for herself from housework because of the violence this may provoke from her husband. Women have far fewer leisure choices than men because their choices about the whole of their lives are more restricted by men and male patriarchal control; leisure and paid employment and freedom to walk the streets are seen as important male rights (although not always achieved, it is true) but not as crucial and legitimate female rights because the latter set of rights threatens the former. That is the crux of the matter. Changing women's social position, while amenable to some reforms of the existing system (better Sex Discrimination legislation, changing taxation and benefit entitlement rules, eliminating the worst excesses of sexism from the education system, raising women's pay in employment) requires the kinds of changes which will dramatically affect men's power, lives and rights. Men taking on an equal share of childcare and housework would have consequences for the organization and pay rates of male employment and for the way that systems of production operate as well as implications for our political system, as too would women having equal pay (and associated equal non-economic bargaining power) with men across the whole occupation spectrum. Being prosecuted for sexual harassment would have an impact on men's behaviour in public and private, in terms of a climate in which such harassment was morally as well as legally unacceptable. Women taking on decision-making positions in the public world in large numbers would make a huge difference. This is not because women are morally superior and more caring or peaceloving than men. Some of them self-evidently are not as countries with female prime ministers have found out. But that public political participation will affect what happens in the household too and will of necessity change structures as well as ideologies (for example why does the House of Commons have the kinds of hours incompatible with any kind of family or leisure existence; if half the MPs were women it would change more than the number of toilets). It is not in men's interests to give up political power to women, to stop exercising social control over female sexuality, to share their jobs with women, to take on an equal share in household work or act like parents rather than absentee father landlords, and so these kinds of changes are going to be much more difficult to achieve. This is partly because as Rowbotham (1985) notes, not only men but women too are ambivalent about changes on this scale. Certainly there is no major political party in the UK which is fully committed even to bringing about the kinds of changes in women's position which are possible through reformist strategies, though as Dunleavy and Husbands (1985) have pointed out, women are an electoral constituency which in future all parties will ignore only at their peril. Nevertheless, unless widespread changes in the roles of women and men do take place then we cannot hope that women's lives and men's control over them will alter to the huge extent that is necessary in order to offer women the same kinds of possibilities for leisure that men currently enjoy.

7. Appreciating women's leisure

Much of the discussion in this final chapter has been about how to improve women's leisure, which as the previous seven chapters have shown, is seriously constrained by all manner of factors, most of them traceable to patriarchal and capitalist structure and ideologies. But at the same time it is important to emphasize the strengths and importance of the forms of leisure which women already have recourse to. Women's leisure displays many qualities not often, if ever, found in women's leisure – solidarity with their own sex but in a spirit of friendship and companionship rather than competition or status struggles, an emphasis on caring and on co-operation, a lack of aggression and selfishness, enjoyment of everyday things and happenings, an emphasis on the creative and aesthetic aspects of life, a willingness to include rather than exclude others, greater detachment from consumerist values. There is certainly no future in advocating that women's leisure should become more like men's, if this means women becoming involved in activities which are selfish, hierarchically organized, over-commercialized, aggressive, competitive and focused on rivalry rather than companionship. The only respect in which women's leisure needs to become more like men's is in the recognition that women, like men, have a right to leisure and relaxation away from all forms of work. But not all women's leisure should or needs to take place in single sex groups and settings, although these are clearly very important to women's freedom. Leisure is after all partly a matter for personal choice and that does and must include the choice of with whom (if anyone) that leisure is shared, as well as what is involved. The context in which companions and activities are chosen, and the provision from which choices are made do need to be changed. With Eisenstein (1984) I do not believe that the road to women's liberation lies along the path of retreat into a solely female world, appealing as that may be, but rather lies in trying to change the existing world both by women organizing autonomously *and* becoming involved in alliances with other groups which include men, whether these are in the trade union movement, political parties, sports clubs or groups working outside the formal political structure. This means as Eisenstein recognizes, both that 'organisations and individuals could eventually be infused with a feminist vision, and a feminist set of issues and priorities' (p. 144) but also

> sharing some . . . political goals . . . associating feminism with the liberating tradition of Western thought, from Locke and Rousseau to Marx and Engels, tending in the direction of greater equality, shared decision-making, and justice. But . . . transforming these traditions, by imbuing them with . . . woman-centred values . . . as necessary and legitimate goals of political life. (Eisenstein, 1984, p. 144–5).

It is my hope that this book has shown the importance of including the right to leisure (or more play, less work) in the demands for women's liberation, as well as contributing to an appreciation of women's lives and leisure as they now exist.

Bibliography

Aldred, C. (1981). *Women at work*. Pan Books.

Anderson, A. (1985). 'Conceptualising and researching the work-leisure complex', paper given to 'Women, leisure and well-being' conference, Dunfermline College of P.E., 19th–21st April.

Arnot, M. (1984). 'How shall we educate our sons?', in Deem, R., (ed.) *Co-education Reconsidered*. Open University Press.

Barrett, M. and McIntosh, M. (1985). 'Ethnocentrism and socialist–feminist theory', *Feminist Review*, No. 20, June, pp 23–47.

Beechey, V. and Perkins, T. (1986). *A Matter of Hours*. Polity Press.

Bell, C. and McKee, L. (1984). 'His unemployment; her problem', paper given to British Sociological Association Conference, University of Bradford, April.

Bell, C. and Roberts, H. (1984). *Social Researching: politics, problem, practice*. Routledge and Kegan Paul.

Berk, R. and S. F. (1979). *Labour and Leisure at Home*. Sage.

Bowles, G. and Duelli Klein, R. (1983). *Theories of Womens Studies*. Routledge and Kegan Paul.

Brittain, V. (1979). *Testament of Youth*. Virago.

Brittain, V. (1980). *Testament of Experience*. Virago.

Brittan, A. and Maynard, M. (1984). *Sexism, racism and oppression*. Blackwells.

Brock, P., (1985). 'Learning to live without a job', the *Guardian*, p. II, May 29th.

Brown, W. (1985). 'Young people and leisure', unpublished report for Milton Keynes Youth Council.

Brownfield Pope, Y. (1985). 'The welfare rights worker's tale'. in Turner, J. and Jardine, B., (eds). *Pioneer Tales: a new life in Milton Keynes*. Peoples Press.

Brownmiller, S. (1975). *Against our will; men, women and rape*. Simon and Schuster.

Bruegel, I. (1983), 'Rejoinder to Bernard Corry, Jim Nugent and David Saunders'. in Evans, M. and Ungerson, C. (eds.) *Sexual Divisions–Patterns and Processes*. Tavistock.

Burgoyne, J. (1985). 'Unemployment and married life', *Unemployment Unit Bulletin*. November 1985, Issue 18, pp 7–10.

Burns, T. (1973). 'Leisure in industrial society, in Smith, M., Parker, S. and Smith, C. (eds.) *Leisure and Society in Britain*, Allen Lane.

Butler, L. (1981). 'GCE for adults; a case of conflicting mythologies'. *Adult Education*, pp 297–304.

Campbell, B. (1984). *Wigan Pier Revisited*. Virago.

Carrington, B. and Leaman, O. (1983). 'Work for some and sport for all', *Youth and Policy*. Vol No I, Issue 3, pp 10–15.

Cavendish, R. (1982). *Women on the line*. Routledge and Kegan Paul.

Chambers, D. (1985). Contribution to 'Women, leisure and well-being' conference, Dunfermline college of P.E., 19–21st April.

Chappell, H. (1982). 'The family life of the unemployed'. *New Society* 4th October, pp 76–9.

Clark, D. (1984). 'Continuity or change; household work strategy of redundant shiftworkers', paper given to British Sociological Association Conference, University of Bradford, April.

Clarke, J. and Critcher, C. (1985). *The Devil Makes Work; Leisure in capitalist Britain.* Macmillan.

Coote, A. and Campbell, B. (1982). *Sweet Freedom.* Pan Books.

Cowie, S. and Lees, S. (1981). 'Slags or drags', *Feminist Review.* Autumn issue.

Coyle, A. (1984). *Redundant Women.* Women's Press.

Cragg, A. and Dawson, T. (1984). 'Unemployed women; a study of attitudes and experiences', Department of Employment Research Paper, No 47.

Crompton, R., Jones, G. and Reid, S. (1982). 'Contemporary clerical work; a case study of local government' in West. J. (ed.), *Women, work and the labour market.* Routledge and Kegan Paul.

Dabrowski, I. (1984). 'The social integration of working class women; a review of employment, voluntary organization and related sex-role literature', *American Journal of Sociology.*

Davidoff, L. (1979). 'The separation of home and work', in Burman, S. (ed.). *Fit work for women.* Croom Helm.

Deem, R. (ed.), (1980). *Schooling for Women's work.* Routledge and Kegan Paul.

Deem, R. (1982a). 'Women, leisure and inequality', *Leisure Studies,* pp 29–46, Vol I, no I, January, pp 29–46.

Deem, R. (1982b). 'Women's leisure – does it exist?', unpublished paper given to 1982 BSA conference, University of Manchester.

Deem, R. (1983). 'Gender, class and patriarchy in the popular education of women', in Walker, S. and Barton, L. (eds.), *Gender, Class and Education.* Falmer.

Deem, R. (1984). (ed.), *Co-education Reconsidered.* Open University Press.

Deem, R. (1985a). 'Leisure, work and unemployment; old traditions and new boundaries', in Deem, R. and Salaman, G. (eds.), *Work, Culture and Society.* Open University Press.

Deem, R. (1985b). 'Lost Horizons', *Sport and Leisure.* July/August, pp 30–1.

Deem, R. (1986). 'Bringing gender equality to the school', paper presented to International Sociology of Education Conference, Westhill College, Birmingham, January.

Deem, R. and Salaman, G. (1985). (eds.), *Work, Culture and Society.* Open University Press.

Delphy, C. (1984). *Close To Home; a materialist analysis of women's oppression.* Hutchinson/Explorations in Feminism Collective.

Dex, S. (1985). *The Sexual division of Work.* Harvester Press.

Dixey, R. and Talbot, M. (1982). 'Women, leisure and bingo'. Trinity and All Saints College, Leeds.

Dobash, R. and R. (1980). *Violence against wives; a case against the patriarchy.* Open Books.

Doust, D. (1982). 'A private battle', *Sunday Times,* May 2nd, cited in Graydon, J. (1983). 'But it's more than a game. It's an institution; Feminist perspectives on sport', *Feminist Review,* Issue 2, Summer.

Duelli Klein, R. (1983). 'Thoughts about feminist methodology' in Bowles and Klein (1983), op. cit.

Dunleavy, P. and Husbands, C. (1985). *British Democracy at the Cross Roads.* Allen and Unwin.

Dunning, E. and Sheard, K. (1979). *Barbarians, Gentlement and Players.* Martin Robertson.

Duquemin, A. (1982). 'Women outside marrige', paper given to British Sociological Association Conference, University of Manchester, April.

Dyer, K. (1982). *Catching up the men.* Junction Books.

Edgell, S. (1982). *Middle Class Couples.* Allen and Unwin.

Eisenstein, H. (1984). *Contemporary Feminist Thought.* Allen and Unwin.

Executive Life Style (1985). anonymous article 'Residents are happier now', p. 16, June issue.

Fagin, L. and Little, M. (1984). *The Forsaken Families.* Penguin.

Featherstone, M. and Hepworth, I. (1981). 'Ageing and inequality; consumer culture and the new middle age', paper given to 1981 BSA conference, University of Aberystwyth.

Feldberg, R. and Glenn, E. N. (1984). 'Male and Female; job versus gender models in the sociology of work', in Siltanen, J. and Stanworth, M. (eds.), *Women in the Public Sphere.* Hutchinson.

Fergusson, R. and Mardle, R. (1981). 'Education and the political economy of leisure' in Dale, R. et al. (eds.). *Education and the State.* Vol II, *Politics Patriarchy and Practice.* Falmer.

Ferris, L. (1981). 'Attitudes to women in sport; prolegomena towards a sociological theory' *Equal Opportunities International.* Vol I, no. 2, pp 32–39.

Finch, J. (1983a). 'Dividing the rough and the respectable; working class women and pre-school playgroups', in Gamarnikov, E., Morgan, D., Purvis, J. and Taylorson, D. (eds.). *The Public and the Private*. Heinemann.

Finch, J. (1983b). *Married to the job*. Allen and Unwin.

Finch, J. (1984). 'Its great to have someone to talk to; the ethics and politics of interviewing women', in Bell, and Roberts, *op cit.*

Finch, J. (1985). *Research and Policy; The uses of qualitative methods in social and educational research*. Falmer Press.

Finch, J. and Groves, D. (1983). *A Labour of Love*. Routledge and Kegan Paul.

Finnegan, R. (1985). 'Working outside formal employment' in Deem and Salaman, *op cit.*

Fitzjohn, M. and Tungatt, M. (1985). 'How to attract women', *Sport and Leisure*. May/June, pp 34–5.

Fletcher, S. (1984). *Women First; the female tradition in English Physical Education 1880–1980*. Athlone Press.

Freedman, P. (1984). 'The fastest painted lady in the world', *Sunday Times Magazine*, May 27th.

French, J. and P. (1984). 'Sociolinguistics and gender divisions' in S.Acker, J. Megarry, S. Nisbet and E. Hoyle, (eds.). *World Year Book of Education 1984; Women and Education*. Kogan Page.

Gamarnikov, E., Morgan, D., Purvis, J. and Taylorson, D. (1983). (eds.). *The Public and the Private*. Heinemann.

Garnsey, E., Rubery, J. and Wilkinson, F. (1985). 'Labour market structures and work force divisions' in Deem and Salaman *op cit.*

General Household Survey 1981. HMSO.

Glyptis, S. (1985). 'The freedom trap', *Sport and Leisure*, May/June, pp 27–8.

Glyptis, S. and Chambers, D. A. (1982). 'No place like home', *Leisure Studies*, Vol I, pp 247–262.

Graham, H. (1983). 'Do her answers fit his questions? Women and the survey method', in E. Gamarnikov, Morgan, D., Purvis, J. and Taylorson, D. (eds.) op cit.

Graham, H. (1984). *Women, health and the family*. Harvester Press.

Gray, A. 'The working class family as an economic unit' in Harris, C. (ed.). *The Sociology of the Family*. Sociological Review Monograph 28.

Graydon, J. (1983). 'But it's more than a game; It's an institution; Feminist perspectives on sport'. *Feminist Review*, Issue 2, pp00–00.

Green, E. and Hebron, S. (1985). presentation given to Women, wellbeing and Leisure Workshop', Dunfermline College of P.E., April.

Green, E., Hebron, S. and Woodward, D. (1985a). 'A Woman's work', *Sport and Leisure*, July/August, pp 36–8.

Green, E., Hebron, S. and Woodward, D. (1985b). 'Leisure and Gender; women's opportunities, perceptions and constraints', unpublished report to ESRC/Sports Council Steering Group, January.

Gregory, S. (1982). 'Women among others: another view'. *Leisure Studies*. Vol I, no I, pp 47–52.

Griffin, C. (1981). 'Young Women and leisure', in Tomlinson, A. (ed.), *Leisure and Social Control*, Brighton Polytechnic, School of Human Movement.

Griffin, C. (1985). *Typical Girls*. Routledge and Kegan Paul.

Grigson, V. (1985). 'Gender specific–injury time' *Sport and Leisure*, July/August, p 55.

Hakim, C. (1981). 'Job segregation trends in the 1970s', *Employment Gazette*. December, pp 521–29.

Hall, C. (1982). 'The butcher, the baker, the candlestick maker; the shop and the family in the Industrial Revolution', in E. Whitelegg et al (ed.) *The Changing Experience of Women*. Martin Robertson.

Hanmer, J. and Maynard, M. (1986). *Women, Violence and Social Control*. Macmillan.

Hargreaves, J. (1985). 'Their own worst enemies', *Sport and Leisure*, July/August, pp 20–8.

Harris, M. (1985). 'Costa del Butlins', *New Society*, August 9th, pp 185–6.

Hayes, J. and Nuttman, P. (1981). *Understanding the Unemployed*. Tavistock.

Hill, J. (1978). 'The psychological impact of unemployment', *New Society*, January 19th, p 19.

Hobson, D. (1981). 'Young women at home and leisure', in A. Tomlinson (ed.), *Leisure and Social Control*. Brighton Polytechnic, pp 134–155.

Holly, L. 1985). 'Feminist Methods in the study of middle class wives and mothers', unpublished paper to Feminist Methods workshop, Open University, Milton Keynes,

October.
Horne, J. (1985). 'What's so new about the new vocationalism? The State and unemployed youth in the Interwar period', in Walker, S. and Barton, L. (eds.). *Youth, unemployment and schooling*. Open University Press.
Hunt, P. (1980). *Gender and Class Consciousness*. Macmillan.
Jenkins, C. and Sherman, B. (1979). *The Collapse of Work*. Eyre Methuen.
Jenkins, C. and Sherman, B. (1981). *The Leisure Shock*. Eyre Methuen.
Jerrome, D. (1983). 'Lonely women in a friendship club'. *British Journal of Guidance and Counselling*, Vol II, No I, pp 10–20.
Kelly, J. (1981). 'Leisure interaction and the Social Dialectic', *Social Forces*, Vol 60, pp 304–332.
Kerr, M. and Charles, N. (1986). 'Servers and providers: the distribution of food within the family'. *Sociological Review*, No 34, Vol I.
Land, I. (1981). 'Parity begins at home; women's and men's work in the home and its effects on their paid employment', SSRC/EOC Research Review.
Leaman, O. (1984). *Sit on the Sidelines and Watch the Boys Play: Sex Differentiation in Physical Education*. Longmans/Schools Council.
Lees, S. (1985). 'Schooling for what? The neglect of gender in subcultural studies'. Unpublished paper given to Westhill Sociology of Education Conference, Birmingham.
Leonard, D. (1980). *Sex and Generation*. Tavistock.
Liddington, J. (1984). *The life and times of a respectable rebel*. Virago.
Liddington, J. and Norris, J. (1978). *One Hand Tied Behind Us*. Virago.
Llewellyn Davies, M. (1904). *The Women's Co-operative Guild 1883–1904*. Kirby Lonsdale.
Llewellyn Davies, M. (1977). *Life as we have known it – by Co-operative Working Women*. Virago.
Llewellyn Davies, M. (1978). *Maternity; letters from working women*. Virago.
Luxton, M. (1980). *More than a Labour of Love*. The Women's Educational Press (Toronto).
McCabe, T. (1981). 'Girls and leisure' in A. Tomlinson (ed.). *Leisure and Social Control*. Brighton Polytechnic.
McIntosh, S. (1981). 'Leisure studies and women' in A. Tomlinson (ed.). ibid.
McLaren, A.T. (1982). 'Ambition and accounts; a study of working class women in adult education', *Psychiatry*. pp 235–246, Vol 45, No. 3.
McRobbie, A. (1978). 'Working class girls and the culture of femininity' in Womens Studies Group, Centre for Contemporary Cultural Studies. *Women Take Issue*. Hutchinson.
McRobbie, A. and McCabe, T. (1981). (eds.). *Feminism for girls*. Routledge and Kegan Paul.
McRobbie, A. and Nava, M. (1984). (eds.). *Gender and Generation*. Macmillan.
Malos, E. (1980). *The Politics of Housework*. Allison and Busby.
Marsden, D. (1981). *Workless*. Croom Helm.
Marshall, G. (1984). 'On the sociology of women's unemployment, its neglect and significance'. *Sociological Review*, Vol 32, pp 235–59.
Martin, J. and Roberts, C. (1984). *Women and Employment; a Lifetime Perspective*. HMSO/Department of Employment.
Martin, R. and Wallace, J. (1984). *Working Women in Recession*. Oxford University Press.
Maynard, M. (1985). 'Houseworkers and their work' in Deem and Salaman (eds.) op cit.
Murcott, A. (1983). 'It's a pleasure to cook for him', in Gamarnikov, E. *et al*. op cit.
Mutrie, N. (1985). 'Women and exercise' paper given to Dunfermline 'Women, wellbeing and leisure' workshop, Dunfermline College of P.E., April.
New Earnings Survey 1984. Department of Employment, HMSO.
Oakley, A. (1981). 'Interviewing women; a contradiction in terms', in Roberts, H. (ed.) *Doing Feminist Research*. Routledge and Kegan Paul.
O'Brien, M. (1982). 'The working father' in Beail, N. and McGuire, J. (eds.). *Fathers; Psychological perspectives*. Junction Books.
Oliver, J. (1982). 'The caring wife' in Finch and Groves, op cit.
Orbach, S. (1982). *Fat is a feminist issue*.
Owen, L. and Lustig, R. (1985). 'Are women closing the gap?'. *The Observer*, Sunday 12th August, p 9.
Pahl, J. (1982). 'The allocation of money and the structuring of inequality within marriage' unpublished paper, Health Services Research Unit, University of Kent.
Pahl, J. (1985). 'Household budgeting' paper given to 'Women, wellbeing and leisure' Workshop, Dunfermline College of P.E., April.
Pahl, R. (1985). *Divisions of Labour*. Blackwells.

Parker, R.S. (1981). 'Change, flexibility, spontaneity and self-determination in leisure, *Social Forces*, Vol 60, No 2, pp 323–331.

Parker, S. (1971). *The Future of Work and Leisure*. MacGibbon and Kee.

Parker, S. (1976). *The Sociology of Leisure*. Allen and Unwin.

Parker, T. (1983). *The People of Providence*. Hutchinson.

Parry, N. and Johnson, D. (1974). 'Sexual divisions and lifestyle' unpublished paper given to BSA Conference, University of Aberdeen.

Pearson, L. (1978). 'Non-work time; a review of the literature' Centre for Urban and Regional Studies, University of Birmingham, Research Memorandum No. 65.

Perkins, T. (1983). 'A new form of employment; a case study of women's part-time work in Coventry', in Evans, M. and Ungerson, C. (eds.). *Sexual Divisions; patterns and processes*. Tavistock.

Poggi, D. and Coormaert, M. (1974). 'The city; off-limits to women', *Liberation*. July/August.

Pollert, A. (1981). *Girls, Wives, Factory Lives*. Macmillan.

Rapoport, R. and R. (1975). *Leisure and the Family Life Cycle*. Routledge and Kegan Paul.

Rapoport, R. and R. (1976). *Dual-Career Families Re-examined*. Martin Robertson.

Rapoport, R. and R. (1978). *Working Couples*. Routledge and Kegan Paul.

Roberts, H. (1981). *Doing Feminist Research*. Routledge and Kegan Paul.

Roberts, K. (1981). *Leisure*. Longmans.

Rojek, C. (1985). *Capitalism and Leisure Theory*. Tavistock.

Rowbotham, S. (1985). ' "What do women want?"; women centred values and the world as it is', *Feminist Review*, No. 20, pp 49–69.

Russell, G. (1983). *The Changing Role of Fathers*. Open University Press.

Scraton, S. (1985). 'Boys muscle in where angels fear to tread; the relationship between physical education and young women's subcultures', paper given to Leisure Studies Association Conference, Ilkley, 12–14th April.

Scraton, S. (1986). 'Images of femininity and the teaching of girls' physical education', in Evans, J. (ed.). *Physical Education; Sport and Schooling*.

Sharpe, S. (1984). *Double Identity*. Penguin.

Siltanen, J. and Stanworth, M. (eds.) (1984). *Women and the Public Sphere*. Hutchinson.

Smart, C. (1984). *The ties that bind*. Routledge and Kegan Paul.

Smith, M., Parker, S. and Smith, C. (1973) (eds.). *Leisure and Society in Britain*. Allen Lane, The Penguin Press.

Social Trends 1985 (1985). OPCS, HMSO.

Spender, D. (1981). *Man Made Language*. Routledge and Kegan Paul.

Spender, D. (1982). *Invisible Women; The Schooling Scandal*. Women's Press.

Sport and Leisure (1985). 'Getting Even', a special All Women issue, July/August.

Stacey, M. (1975). *Power, persistence and change*. Routledge and Kegan Paul.

Stanley, L. (1980). 'The problem of women and leisure – an ideological construct and a radical feminist alternative' paper given to the 'Leisure in the 80s' Forum, sponsored by Capital Radio, London, 26th–28th September.

Stanley, L. (1985). 'The methodology of women's leisure', presentation to Dunfermline College of P.E. 'Women, wellbeing and Leisure' workshop, April.

Stanley, L. and Wise, S. (1983). *Breaking Out*. Routledge and Kegan Paul.

Stamp, P. (1985). 'Research note; balance of financial power in marriage; an exploratory study of breadwinning wives, *Sociological Review*, August, Vol 33, No 3, pp 540–557.

Szalai, A. (1972). *The Use of Time*. Mouton, The Hague.

Talbot, M. (1979). *Women and Leisure; A state of the Art review*. SSRC/Sports Council.

Talbot, M. (1981). 'Women and sport – social aspects'. *Journal of BioSocial Science*. Supplement 7, pp 33–47.

Talbot, M. (1984). 'Women and sport; a contradiction in terms' paper presented to International Conference of the Leisure Studies Association, University of Sussex, July.

Thompson, E.P. (1967). 'Time, work-discipline and industrial capitalism'. *Past and Present*, No. 38, December.

Thompson, J. (1983). *Learning Liberation*. Croom Helm.

Tomlinson, A. (1979). *Leisure and the role of clubs and voluntary groups*. SSRC/Sports Council. 1979. London.

Tomlinson, A. (1981). *Leisure and Social Control*. Brighton Polytechnic.

Turner, J. and Jardine, B. (1985). *Pioneer Tales*. The Peoples Press.

Tysoe, M. (1985). 'Tourism is good for you'. *New Society*, 16th August 1985, pp 228–230.

Ungerson, C. (1983). 'Women and caring; skills, tasks and taboos', in Gamarnikov et al. op. cit.

Wallace, C. (1985). 'Masculinity, femininity and unemployment'. Walker, S. and Barton, L. (eds.). *Youth, Unemployment and Schooling.* Open University Press.

Walker, D. (1985). 'The Architect's Tale', in Turner and Jardine, op. cit.

Walker, K.E. and Woods, M. (1976). 'Time use; a measure of household production of family goods and services'. American Home Economics Association.

Walker, S. and Barton, L. (1985). (eds.). *Youth, Unemployment and Schooling.* Open University Press.

Weiner, G. (ed.) (1985). *Just a Bunch of Girls.* Open University Press.

West, J. (1982). 'New technology and women's office work'. in West, J. (ed.). *Women, work and the Labour market.* Routledge and Kegan Paul.

Westwood, S. (1984). *All Day, Every Day.* Pluto.

Wickham, A. (1986). *Women and Training.* Open University Press.

Willis, P. (1985). 'Not to Labour; cultural and policy considerations of youth unemployment'. Unpublished paper given to Westhill Sociology of Education Conference.

Wimbush, E. (1985). 'Conceptualising and researching the work-leisure complex'. 'Women, wellbeing and leisure' Workshop, Dunfermline College of P.E., April.

Wood, S. (1981). 'Redundancy and female employment' *Sociological Review,* Vol 29, No. 4.

Woodward, D. (1985). 'Survey of leisure providers'. 'Women, well-being and leisure' Workshop, Dunfermline College of P.E.

Wyatt, S. (1985). 'Science Policy Research Unit; Time Budget Studies'. ibid.

Index